Learning

Self Help Guide on How to Learn Faster and
Remember Anything

(Advanced Learning Strategies to Boost
Brainpower and Focus)

Alistair H. Young

Published by Rob Miles

Accelerated Learning: Self Help Guide on How to Learn Faster and Remember Anything (Advanced Learning Strategies to Boost Brainpower and Focus)

ISBN 978-1-7771171-5-3

Legal & Disclaimer

Table of Contents

Introduction

As human beings, we are always learning new skills and additional information. Our brains are geared to constantly be adding to our store of knowledge. The data collected from our senses is filtered and analyzed based on what we already know about a specific topic. Our life experiences also play a part in how we analyze and classify or filter new information. The question for teachers, trainers and others within various organizations is how to maximize our brain's ability to take in new information and process it quickly. By doing so, organizations find that they can train their workers to execute new skills faster, thus saving time and money in the long run.

While we are always taking in new data, we might always understand what is being presented. Therefore, a critical part of learning any new skill or task is to be able to then execute the skill or task properly with minimal practice or additional training. There are those who spend their lives studying how we learn and then execute based on what we learn. These researchers have come up with an effective way to teach students, workers and even management through a process called Accelerated Learning.

But what is Accelerated Learning? What is involved in creating an Accelerate Learning program tailored to your needs or the needs of your company or school? In this book, we will explore Accelerated Learning, how it works and most importantly, how you can put it into practice by means of guideposts and other methods. So let's start by learning a bit more about what Accelerate Learning really is all about, particularly in terms of what it means for teachers and students.

Chapter 1: The 'What' Of NLP

To put it simply, NLP is a scientific technique, involving the usage and optimization of three components of the human system, i.e. neurology, linguistics and programming.

The NLP techniques were first implemented in 1970 by two gentlemen, going by the names of John Grinder and Richard Bandler. The primary focus of Neuro Linguistic Programming (henceforth referred to as NLP) is to tap into the hidden potential of the human brain, expanding its capacities beyond the conventional horizons.

It is no secret that the human brain is capable of storing and recording vast quantities of data, information and knowledge, enabling the human kind to achieve goals with ease. However, this is not quite true, as proven by innumerous people excelling admirably in particular fields while simultaneously failing in other fields. For example, it is quite a common phenomenon for a professional prodigy to have poor personal relations, and a societal person to lack the energy left to perform well professionally.

The sole purpose of NLP is to channelize the energies latent within the human mind towards a more productive goal, by decoding the interaction between the thought processes ongoing in the mind (neuro), the way these thought processes are expressed by us (linguistics) and the reactions and behavior displayed in similar arising situations (programming). By doing so, NLP helps making the completion and achievement of goals an easier task.

We all know, oftentimes our thoughts and actions differ widely. Our plans either are performed with poor execution, or we lack the punctuality to perform them in time. Some guidance is thereby required in order to synchronize our thoughts and actions by modifying our behavior to suit the conditions faced. It strategizes our mind to stay focused on the task at hand, in a world where multitasking is quickly becoming the most accepted trend.

Chapter 2: Memory Is A Habit

Imagine you were in a game show and that you are on the last question. This is IT! One correct answer and you'd win a billion dollars. And the question, when it is asked, takes you by surprise because it is quite simple – what's your social security number or better yet, what's your pin code?

Quite a lot of people you know (possibly yourself including) may have just missed the fortune of a lifetime if such a question were asked. Why did that happen?

As children, we are in awe of the world. We love to learn new things. Many times, we want to impress adults or love to have fun with some numbers. So, we find delight in learning things that seem tricky – like a list of 10 phone numbers or a really long list of groceries.

As we grow older, we lose quite a bit of this wonder-filled, child-like awe for numbers, names and words, among other things. We're not so much concerned with impressing others anymore. In any case, where's the time? More important matters take precedence over interesting yet time-consuming mind games that tickle the remote corners of the brain.

This is the first stage of atrophy.

If you've ever made the remark 'I just can't seem to remember – could be my age', you know exactly what I'm talking about. It has been scientifically proven that in over 74% cases, memory has not really declined when the individual complains that it has.

Then, why do we forget?

According to scientists, the brain wasn't designed to store reams of data for a long time unless you make a concentrated effort to store it. For instance, boring but essential data like addresses, appointments, telephone numbers, social security numbers – even anniversaries and birthdays – have a short shelf life in the brain.

If you really want to remember information that is not very special or exciting, which most training courses and study material faithfully add up to, you have to make a conscious effort to do so.

Otherwise, your short-term memory will just flush it out.

And there you were blaming your age for your own laziness!

You may very well be carrying the most advanced microchip in the world between your ears, but even your brain tends to get rusty if it is not used optimally. Typically, this is what happens as we age.

If brains were super-computers, you could simply perform an upgrade as you got older by adding a chip. But upgrading the human memory takes slightly more effort, as I'm sure you'd agree.

First of all, let's go to the basic question: What is memory? The simplest definition for memory would be 'a mental activity for recalling information that has been learned or experienced'.

So, your memory is all about the three R's:
• Receiving,
• Retaining and
• Retrieving data.

Concentration plays an important part in learning and recovering data. For example, suppose you have been using the same route to get to your office for the last 10 years, and someone suddenly asks you about a shop in one of the blocks you pass by – would you know it?

If you do not pay attention to a piece of information consciously for at least 8-10 seconds, it will not impinge on your brain. Even so, it will get written only on your short term memory – so, you'd still not remember the name of that shop. That name may be dancing wickedly on the tip of your tongue, refusing to fall out. Here, you have the classic retrieval problem.

What happened? You have received the data and retained it but you don't know what you've done with it. Your mind is waiting for a cue so that it can access the correct file from the thousands and millions of dusty old files it holds. And you've lost the key.

From the above, it is quite obvious that effective and fast learning happens only when you can file away information systematically and tag it so you know what cues work for which folders. This is a consciously developed habit. Students make use of it daily when they learn questions and corresponding answers. But that kind of learning takes for ever.

So, are learning and memory never affected by external factors?

Yes, they are! Remember, learning takes place in your brain. The brain, like every other organ, needs fuel to function. Therefore, your dietary habits, level of physical fitness and emotional health play an important part in your learning process. Of these, the food you eat directly translates into brain horsepower!

We will be discussing these aspects in detail later on.

Doesn't memory ever decline with age?

Sadly, some forms of memory seem to decline with age. Ageing physical processes could be the reason. As we grow older, blood flow to the brain becomes restricted and there is a short supply of oxygen. Another hypothesis suggests that older people have difficulty filing away information and attaching the correct key to each of these bits and pieces of data. As you know once the key is lost, the data is also – for all practical purposes – lost.

Advancing age has limited impact on the learning process. It can slow you down by 2-3% only.

Learning curves suggest that a lot of the information we take in is lost within 5 minutes of receiving the data. Over 90% - to be exact - is lost within 24 hours. But there are various techniques that help you reverse this curve. Once you learn these techniques, memorizing will become an enjoyable game. The best part is that the storage space in your memory is almost limitless. You really cannot learn enough to choke your memory. And the more you learn, the better your memory gets.

The good news is memory can be taught. So, you can teach yourself to receive more data and retrieve all of it. Surprising as that may sound that's exactly what memory stunts are all about.

Maybe you didn't know this, but memory can be bought too. Certain food products and herbs, if taken in proper doses, enhance your ability to memorize. Certain physical exercises can also help. We'll be getting to that later in the book.

The techniques you're about to learn focus on every stage of the process called learning. The method in which you take in data, the way in which you store it and the process you use to retrieve it will decide the speed of memorizing. You can learn a long speech, memorize a big list or even quote Shakespeare – you can do just about anything when you make use of these advanced learning techniques.

So remember, memory is just a habit. If you've lately got into the habit of memorizing less, don't worry. It's just a question of jogging your mental processes to accept, store and recover more data.

Chapter 2.0 Recap:
• Memory is **R**eceiving, **R**etaining and **R**etrieving   data.
• More than **90%** of what we learn is lost within 24 hours of learning IF there are no follow-up methods used to retain data.
• Memory deteriorates with **age**, but it deteriorates faster due to **neglect**.

- You can **teach** yourself to learn faster and memorize more.

Chapter 3: IQ Increasing Techniques

In this chapter, you will learn proven, time-tested, and recognized techniques to increase your intelligence quotient. But first, are you conscious that your IQ is determined by two factors? Only fifty percent can be credited to genetics. The rest is actually up to you and how you will increase it. There are ways to improve your IQ. Some of these are described in this section.

Maintain a Sound Body and Mind

You can increase your IQ if you take conscious efforts to keep your heart well. Every now and then, you should do some conscious effort to raise your heart rate. Also, breaking perspiration is a good idea if you wish to combat loss of memory. Actions like jogging, riding a bike, playing sports, and swimming are helpful in improving one's mind. This helps in the delivery of enough oxygen to the brain. If you do this regularly, your brain functions will be better and this will aid you to deal with pressure well. In result, your IQ score will be a lot better.

Write, Write, Write

If you are a writer, you are very fortunate. You get to increase your brain capabilities on a regular basis. Do you recall when you were still in school? You tend to write everything. That is really a good exercise because it increases your IQ. It helps you because it aids you to recall the details of what you write.

So, if you are not a writer, you can still write frequently. Perhaps, you can keep a journal or a diary. This will give you a venue to jot down every idea, every thought, and every event that you desire to remember. But do not stop at writing them down. On a daily basis, try to read them again. The review procedure will help you because it increases your brain's retention capability.

Did you know that the most popular geniuses of all time like Isaac Newton, Thomas Jefferson, and Albert Einstein all have journals? Also, they were careful to be compulsive writers in their journals.

Maybe that would motivate you to keep one.

Avoid boredom by all means

Being a couch potato is a sign of boredom. So, you should leave excessive TV viewing. Mom was correct when she told you that TV can make you dumb.

Instead of surfing through your TV channels or lying idly on your bed, why not resolve a crossword puzzle? If you have a chess set, try playing against yourself. Improve your logical capabilities by keeping your hands full and never falling into the attraction of boredom.

Purchase that Rubik's Cube

What barbells are to muscles is what Rubik's cube is to the brain. You should thank the man who created it in 1974. That crucial year in Hungary, Erno Rubik was able to create a toy that made thousands of people smarter. The Rubik's cube can increase your capability in geometry and visualize 3D figures. Tease your brain regularly because the Rubik's cube gives you a unique arrangement to be solved every single time!

Embrace the beauty of being a lifelong learner

You should be open to learning something new every single day of your life. Learning does not stop at school. But most of the neural pathways were created when you were at your school age. In order to sustain the progress, you should continuously seek new learning.

Every day, you should try out something new. If possible, enroll yourself in a course. After college, you may also consider enrolling at the Graduate School. This will help you expand the limits of your mind.

Chapter 4: Neural Pathways /Habitual Tendencies

Brain function is affected daily; by many factors, including the environment, drugs, stress, television, learning and aging. We want to not only stop the bad habit that is bringing bad results but to also replaces it with a power habit to accelerate great results. The goal is to become more mindful and aware so we can change our paradigm -"Paradigms are a multitude of habits that guide every move you make. Negative and faulty paradigms are why ninety-some percent of the population keeps getting the same results, year in and year out." -Bob Proctor Some things in life are guaranteed and you can guarantee results based on your power of will.

Concentrated Power of Will

The great secret of any accomplishment is having great will power. Everything Is possible in today's time, the recourses we have access to gives us a chance to live as we desire. We must learn the inner energy that controls all conscious acts. When you master this lesson, you will have a mighty force at your disposal.

Concentration develops determination, perseverance, and directly effects memory. You will experience overall higher attention in the moment. You have as strong a will as anyone but it must be developed and something you continue to work on.

You Can Concentrate, But Are You? Everyone has the ability to concentrate. Pay more attention to detail and what actually needs to be done. Try to catch your self falling out of concentration. That happens often so you'll get a chance to find out what causes that distraction. The amount of attention and concentration you put in on something is ultimately up to you. Great things can become accomplished with the power of concentration yet only few take advantage.

Concentration can make all the difference for massive results and accomplishing our overall purpose. Many things can distract your focus and attention; part of it is what we put in our bodies as we already covered in the previous chapter.

Creating New Habits that Upgrade Your Life

Become cleaner

Being clean and tidy makes you more productive at work. Studies show that people who live and work in clean environments tend to be more focused and productive at work, letting them generate better results and earn more money.

Not only does a clean and tidy living environment make your mind more focused; it also makes it mentally healthier. Cleaning your home, along with other home tasks, can improve your mental health and prevent depression.

Social

Environment

The people you surround yourself with can highly effect your focus and concentration, like-minded groups, are more productive and push each other towards similar goals. Spend your valuable time more efficiently, spend more time around people that you feel a sense of flow towards your overall goals. Maybe spending less time around certain people if necessary because you find your goals don't match up. The key is to spend more time around people that help you and put yourself in environments where you can succeed.

Organize,Routines,Systems

Make routines and become organized, - place your keys in the same place everyday so you never have to waste time looking for them. Create routines to place your keys on the hook when you first walk through the door and place your phone to charge. These routines will become a natural habit.

When you have set and organized items for certain places in your home/office there is a mental picture of where to look first when you need that item. The notes, emails, and documents on your computer should be just as organized as your home for the same reason. If you do anything many times in a day, it would be more productive to make a system for it. For example; If you send the same email to clients many times then create a simple system for each email to be standard for those certain clients.

The busier you are, the more it makes sense to create systems around what you do most often throughout your day. These systems are meant to make your life easier and more practical.

Stop Multi-Tasking

If you take all the to-do's from your head and write them in a to-do list , a wonderful thing happens – suddenly, your mind has 100% resources available and 100% concentration just for the current task at a time. Multitasking can make you less productive.When we try to do more than one thing at a time, our mind can't help but switch on-off the tasks at hand. This results in decreases in attention span, learning, performance, and short-term memory.

Welcome   To   The   Moment
Living   in   the   present
- Do you ever catch yourself worrying or thinking about the future? Become aware of your thoughts. -Begin focusing on what

you're doing now and give this moment your very best. Give your best to people around you, it's very important to be a good listener and it's a great quality to have. Get better at remembering people's names when you meet them for the first time, often it's easy to forget because of the excitement of meeting someone new and racing thoughts. Slow down, breathe and learn to enjoy each and every moment, -tune into the world around you by using all your senses (sights, smell and sounds especially). Worrying about what you have to do later is usually caused by bad time management, procrastination and too busy of a schedule. The best preparation for tomorrow is giving your best today. -H. Jackson Brown, Jr. Talk less Listen more: Begin listening to what people are saying; consider their ideas and try to understand before responding. Use your concentration to focus on what is being said and not what you're going to say next. It's possible for

22

some people to hear but not listen. This means they can't recall anything at all because they were thinking about tomorrow or other plans. Don't interrupt people when they speak and understand the balance of a conversation so that you can give the other person a chance to listen and speak. Think before you speak words are powerful and you must learn to use them effectively. Listening will take some focus and you will see growth in your concentration from active listening.

Promoting Better Brain Memory Functions
Neural pathways are paths or roads through which messages travel. This is where communications between the nerve cells happen. This is also the path taken when creating habits and memories. The more often these pathways are used, the more solid they become. When you first learn, see, hear, or experience something, a neural pathway is created. However, this pathway is also shaky and easily destroyed. That's why some things are easily forgotten.

The more often you think, perform, or experience the same event, the pathway involved solidifies, much like when you are passing through a grassy patch of grounds. The first time you pass through, your path is barely noticeable. As you frequently pass over the same path, it becomes more and more visible. These pathways can be built and changed over time. This is because the brain is a dynamic organ. It allows for changes, creation of the new, and changing of the old. This is called neuroplasticity.

The neuroplasticity of the brain can be improved through exercises. It is similar to how you would improve the function of the different muscles of the brain by engaging in physical exercise. The more often you exercise your brain, the better results you get. This vital organ requires exercise and conditioning just as your heart and the rest of the body require regular exercise.

Rewiring the Brain Through Learning

When we learn a new skill, whether it's Learning golf, doing yoga, expanding your vocabulary or playing an instrument, we are changing how your brain is wired on a deep level. Our brain still has the capability to be rewired even at an older stage of life, it will just take more effort to do so. For example, children soak in information constantly and learn languages much faster. Adults still can learn new languages as well but it will just take more practice.

When we do something repetitive like creative writing over time, you'll see it has become easier to do and remember, we're triggering a pattern of electrical signals through our own neurons. -Practice and repetition make the signals stronger and faster.

Practice Makes Permanent - The more times the network is stimulated, the stronger and more efficient it becomes. Repeating an activity, retrieving a memory, and reviewing material in a variety of ways helps build thicker, stronger, more hard-wired connections in the brain. When people repeatedly practice an activity or access a memory, their neural networks groups of neurons that fire together, creating electrochemical pathways that shape themselves according to that activity or memory.

Using Neuroplasticity to Enhance Memory

Recognizing that learning is essentially the formation of new or stronger neural connections, it makes sense to prioritize activities that help you tap into already-existing pathways.

Here are some exercises you can choose from and practice mental stimulation to enhance your **memory pathways**. Challenge yourself and experience more.

Test Recall

To test your recall ability, write a short list. Try something like a grocery list or your to-do list for the day. Write down things and go over them. Then, memorize the list. After about an hour, try to recall the things you have written on the list. Challenge yourself to recall or call to mind as many items on the list as possible. Make each recall test more challenging than the last one.

Draw a Map Based on Memory

Start by drawing a mental map containing the places you frequently see. Draw a simple map of the route you take from home to work. Then, try to make the map more detailed.

Another exercise is to draw a map right after visiting a new place. Make it as detailed as possible. Perform this every time you go to a new place. This can greatly help your memory and give you a better sense of direction as well.

Mental Math

Calculators are everywhere. People have become so dependent on them that people use these for even simple arithmetic. You can enhance the neural pathways you have made when you were in kindergarten when you first learned to count and perform arithmetic functions. Instead of using a calculator or jotting the numbers down, perform the calculations in your head.

Do a Taste-Buds-Challenge

Notice that you can stimulate your brain and use neuroplasticity even in the simplest daily tasks. Even while you are eating, you can enhance your memory and challenge your brain. Pay more attention to the distinctive taste of the individual ingredients. For example, when eating salad, try to identify what vegetables are in it based on the texture and taste. Drink a smoothie and try to identify the different ingredients, such as what milk was used (i.e. dairy milk, soy milk, etc.), and what sweetener was used (i.e. honey, white sugar, Stevia, etc.).

Learn to Cook

Take cooking classes to learn how to prepare new dishes. When you cook, several senses are stimulated. The sense of smell, taste, sight, and touch are all involved, even in something as simple as cooking eggs. The stimulated senses will, in turn, stimulate different areas of the brain. The more areas are stimulated, the better the brain functioning becomes.

Learn a New Language

Keep challenging your brain by learning a foreign language. Enriching your vocabulary is another great way to lower the risk of cognitive decline. It keeps areas in your brain functioning well, counteracting any degrading effects of factors like stress, drugs, disease and aging. You can even add more words to your vocabulary for your 1st language.

Creating Word Pictures

Word pictures are visualizations of certain words. Think of a word and then spell that word in your head. Don't use auto correct when spelling and try to remember how to spell complicated words. Visualize the words spelled out in your mind.

Motor Skills Grow The Mind

Large and small motor-skill development with both right and left hands is directly linked to development in the left and right hemispheres of the brain. The more movement we can do with our body, hands and feet directly grow the mind.

Play Music

Music is an effective way of enhancing your brain's capacity. Whether it involves playing an instrument or singing in a choir, the effect is remarkable. The process of learning how to play a musical instrument or singing involves a complex set of activities that engages almost every part of the brain.

Playing music especially helps in developing the motor, auditory, and visual cortices. This kind of activity gives the brain a full workout. The activity requires discipline. It involves a structured practice that strengthens several brain functions. For example, playing music will enhance the auditory functions. It helps the auditory area of the brain to be more discerning of the differences in tone and how they create harmony.

This improved focus on hearing can help a person be more attuned or more aware of the sounds around. Also, playing music has been found to be effective in increasing the activity and the size of the brain's corpus callosum. This area connects the brain's left and right hemisphere. This is a vital area that allows different areas of the brain to communicate rapidly and efficiently. Music improves the function of the corpus callosum. It develops the musician's problem-solving abilities, helping with creative and effective ideas. This ability extends beyond the realm of music. It can be useful for social and academic settings too.

Music, playing an instrument or singing, includes creating and gaining an understanding of the message and the emotional content. Engaging in musical activities helps in achieving higher levels in the brain's executive functioning. This includes interlinked tasks such as attention to detail, strategizing and planning. This also involves making an analysis of the emotional and cognitive aspects.

All these have an impact on the functioning of the memory systems. Musicians display enhanced memory capabilities. They are more efficient and quicker at creating and storing memories, as well as in retrieving them. Their brains are highly connected that it is able to make interconnected tags on memories, such as emotional tag, contextual, audio and conceptual tags. It works like a very efficient search engine that provides a more complete picture of a memory, rather than fragmented ones.

Refining Hand-Eye Coordination

Engage in activities that require hand-eye coordination. Examples are hobbies that use fine motor skills. For instance; drawing, tennis or painting.

Learning a new sport- Athletic exercises not only work out the muscles, but these also work out the brain tissues. Choose sports that involve using the body and the mind, such as sports like tennis, yoga and golf. The hands grow the mind, learn to use both hands and become strongly coordinated.

Improving Penmanship

It is never too late to practice and improve your penmanship. Writing, in general, helps build important neural pathways in the brain, helping you to better remember whatever you are recording.

Also, writing in cursive style is better than print when learning, children have an easier time first learning cursive writing than print. The flow from cursive is more suited for children with yet underdeveloped finer hand movements compared to writing haltingly with print letters. There is a strong connection to the brain when it comes to writing, in our history, we were depended on writing by hand. Typing on the computer doesn't have the same growing affect as writing.

Brain FIT -Why is it that we set days of the week to work out our bodies but never set aside a day just for brain exercise? You must put in the work to see results. Keep the brain engaged and continue to challenge different areas of the brain just like you would for your body. Today start to add brain exercise to your weekly schedule.

Chapter 5: Strategies to Help Develop a Photographic Memory

A

 photographic memory, or eidetic memory as it is now and again called, is the capacity to see a picture, a scene, or a page just once and later reviewing everything about what was seen without taking a gander at it once more. It is anything but the expertise that everyone has, and the majority of the general population who have this specific capacity are brought into the world with it. Nonetheless, it is conceivable to prepare the cerebrum and upgrade memory aptitudes in any person from the all-inclusive community until they have the practically immaculate review that the vast majority brought into the world with eidetic capacity have.

A great many people feel that eidetic and photographic memory are the equivalent, which isn't generally valid. The eidetic mind is the capacity to see a picture and later review even the smallest subtleties of that picture. This can happen even without appreciating what that picture truly is. A photographic memory is the capacity to consider that similar picture with an ideal understanding of what the subtleties are and what they mean. Notwithstanding, if it is conceivable to build up a photographic memory to the degree of having the option to have eidetic capacity is as yet not indisputably demonstrated.

There are numerous manners by which individuals have attempted to build up their very own recollections to such boundaries, as having such a close flawless memory can be useful to anyone.

Various Strokes for Different Folks

School trains youngsters by methods for having them continue everything, at that point by partner what they realize with different ideas. They are educated in approaches to enable them to recollect data all the more effectively. For example, to recall what certain expressions or words mean, they are trained to utilize them in sentences and short stories. You can say they build up a photographic memory of those words by affiliation.

Many individuals experience difficulty reviewing numbers and sets of numbers. They are probably the hardest things to recollect. Individuals who have figured out how to create photographic recollections probably won't need to connect names with pictures; however, have a kind of capacity bank inside their cerebrums where they document data identified with numbers.

More than one examination has demonstrated that eidetic memory, not to be mistaken for photographic memory, is unprovable. Anyway, there are speculations which express that youngsters may have some eidetic memory which is lost as they become more seasoned. It is conceivable to prepare the cerebrum to a limited degree, potentially even to build up a photographic memory. The strategies used to make can be changed and extraordinary. The fact of the matter is if your favored technique is completed long enough, you will encounter a lift in memory control.

Double the Reading Speed and Astonish Others

People some of the time get disappointed because they fall behind when perusing and learning because of the enormous measures of reading material they should assimilate for school or work. Such vast numbers of books are being composed around the world, that perusers in some cases experience issues staying aware of the generation of fiction and true to life works. It tends to be genuinely stunning, attempting to stay informed of everything " don't you think.

In the expediently changing and exceedingly focused business world, with new items and administrations, and new redesigns presented each week, speed perusing indeed proves to be useful. Most corporate moguls presently examined a few business-related books each week. That is a great deal of work for those unfortunates who don't have speed perusing capacities.

Speed Reading empowers people adolescent ought to be taken in up to multiple times or 3 x whatever they generally contemplate inside once.

Perusing analysts recently decided the intellectual capacities are fit for understanding and inventorying through ten,500 to 60,000 models of information each minute. Along the unit is a roughly single word. The body's five sentiments are receptors for subtleties, which as a rule this gets in the specific profundities of the mind-brain to be recorded concerning posterity. When the mindful musings need nuances, it is have been in the oblivious. Next, it surfaces the necessary information concerning running and utilizes, like your PC.

A decent correspondence is accessible in the middle of the mind, that correctly think about how the PC Computer, and the cerebrum that comprises of emotions and furthermore contemplations. Practically all data will get handled such that we may find it.

The data that people acquire, procedure, and furthermore evaluate begins from our five physical, substantial resources.

Alongside which information, our cerebrum can settle on decisions, decisions, and judgment making. We all find utilizing our own five sentiments (i.at the. locate, smell, perusing, feel, taste), which are already pre-modified to react in a flash.

A genuine case of pre-modified activity: Consider the case of the high schooler kid who scents pizza and what his response is. It is like Pavlov's canine since his faculties make an impression on the mind as an idea.

The impression of inclination our preferred sustenance is a mental exercise, contrasted with the response of gulping, which is physical. In this manner, cerebrum and the brain is the place the activity is, and the body is the place the answer is.

Contemplating this strategy concerning speed considering can inspire the utilization of 3 from the five detects. That is a technique that will firmly impact proper exertion into the recall, recollect and fathom; well beyond in which, properly train you Means of being much better and increasingly effective perusers.

Do as trained, and you'll transform into any speed perusers that want to inspect as improve the gauge of his or her very own living. We accept incredible, decisive triumphs of your stuff with fabulous progressions in a few places you will ever have.

Information: The regular United states secondary schoolmaster (I comprehend this appears to be odd, yet some are graduating without to have the option to learn at an extraordinary eighth quality stage), filters from around 200 terms every single moment. A fantastic understudy peruses 20% quicker with 300 words every single moment. Notwithstanding precisely what your standard or maybe starting examining rate will be, your very own planned scanning speed in the wake of utilizing these sorts of systems will be all the more rapidly in addition to your potential is exceptionally boundless. It is because scientists who have investigated the human cerebrum/mind assent our conceivable is endless. Twofold triple-fourfold your perusing speed, there is just no limitation.

You can hope to figure out how to accomplish your most unique possibilities as a peruser, specialist, understudy, and so on. This is because you're turning into a constant speed peruser and a total accomplishment throughout everyday life.

Be Dynamic Through Speed Reading will enable you to turn out to be boundless in your capacity and capacity to do, be, and have all that you need throughout everyday life, regardless of whether its incredible evaluations or budgetary achievement.

Step by step instructions to Read Better and Faster

Most understudies and experts might want to figure out how to peruse better and quicker to ace more significant volumes of data and invest more energy doing the things they appreciate. When you've never done any examination on the best way to improve your perusing aptitudes, you may accept that it is impossible you can peruse better and quicker because our perusing rates are fixed. If this were valid, at that point everybody would read at a similar speed.

In any case, there is consistently somebody who can peruse preferable and quicker over you, and this is because they have accepted the time and open the door to learn speed examining systems and actualize them in their lives.

Figuring out how to peruse better and quicker through speed, perusing has various points of interest. Above all else, you get the chance to read more sections in far less time, which extends your database and makes you educated about various things. Besides that, you likewise get a more excellent vocabulary, expanded fixation, better relational abilities, and improved fixation and core interest. The best part about figuring out how to peruse better and quicker is that it doesn't take four years of diligent work to get familiar with the procedures to speed perusing. You should put aside, at any rate, ten minutes consistently to rehearse these essential systems, and you will peruse better and quicker in the blink of an eye.

The secret to figuring out how to peruse better and quicker is to maintain a strategic distance from the negative behavior patterns that hinder our scanning speed. One of these is called sub-vocalization - the propensity for perusingg the words so anyone can hear as you read them. Attempt to act naturally mindful when you read, and catch yourself when you discover your lips moving alongside the content. By taking out this propensity, you'll realize how to peruse better and quicker in the blink of an eye. Another of these negative behavior patterns is back-skipping or glancing back at words and sentences you've just scrutinized. Back-skipping, as a rule, happens when the peruser is staring off into space or is just half-centered around the content in front. To keep yourself from back-skipping, ensure you're perusing in a reasonable, agreeable condition free from undesirable diversions. By reading in a spot that is helpful for learning, you'll see that you can understand better and quicker as a result of the expanded concentration and focus.

When you practice how to peruse better and quicker, ensure you work on utilizing a content that is anything but difficult to read. Try not to attempt to improve your speed reading abilities using a confounded specialized manual with bunches of language! The best perusing material to rehearse on is a paper or magazine article on a theme you find fascinating. Like this, you'll have some good times figuring out how to peruse better and quicker, and you'll discover some new information about a point that interests you as well.

You can likewise buy a speed perusing program in case you're not kidding about figuring out how to read better and quicker. Speed perusing projects contain every one of the mysteries and traps to improving as a peruser, and the more significant part of them have unconditional promises if you don't want twofold you're perusing speed. So if showing yourself how to read better and quicker isn't working, consider giving the experts a chance to enable you to out.

Why We Need to Learn Accelerated Learning Techniques

A few teachers would state that the center of quickened learning system is disguising the date with the utilization of the components of life. There is no utilization of power or control to defeat the method. Ordinarily, educators would consolidate life's elements, and they would now be able to bring the most out of the information without getting exhausted by any means. Each understudy is getting a lot of information while learning in an entirely agreeable condition.

In any circumstance, an agreeable physical condition assumes a significant job in learning, particularly when you're applying the procedures of quickened learning. It equips each effort towards making a happy with learning condition for the understudies. The correct temperature, lighting, plants, shade of the divider, the furniture utilizes, and even the design has a significant influence in giving the best happy with learning condition for the understudies.

Different reasons why we have to become familiar with this procedure is because it tells us techniques on the best way to fortify the exercises. A guide to this is the utilization of visual guides or any peripherals that will help animate the intuitive personality while the understudy concentrates his or her eyes on the educator. Visuals help in getting understudies consideration and in this manner, at last, help them adapt rapidly.

Another motivation behind why we have to gain proficiency with this procedure is for us, instructors, to have the option to give the most out of the data and have the opportunity to convey it to the understudies without exhausting them. Instructors are capable of each tyke's learning. When we don't ace this method, we probably won't almost certainly show the children fabulous. The quickened learning procedure encourages us like the correct utilization of our tone. Without the educators' direction, the understudy may think that its difficult to learn and review immense measure of information.

Additionally, another reason is that it's a quick-paced world out there; everybody should be focused to exceed expectations at what they're doing. This can be at school or work. It's concentrate at work as well. You must be speedy at engrossing all data, or else you'll get a reminder and possibly get terminated.

The procedures can help us in any field that we are in. It tends to be utilized at school as well as in our calling. We as a whole need to be focused, and we need to stay aware of what's is happening now. We can beat and embrace current changes in case we're devoted to figuring out how to receive to change and be focused by learning rapidly.

The Benefits of Accelerated Learning Techniques

Quickened learning strategies handle the association between your body and your psyche and will utilize the data from the eyes, ears, and contact to learn. Given by the instructor's comprehension and supervision will help the cerebrum work and license it to develop innovative and imaginative addresses. The answer for effective routine with regards to quickened learning strategies is keeping up the dauntlessness between customary address and non-traditional addresses.

A case of these learning systems incorporates using music to impact the passionate condition and the state of mind of each student. The impact of music can be colossally profitable for an instructor wishing to bond with students on a blend of subjects.

The thoughts of quickened learning likewise comprise of the first convictions of non-cognizant education. The utilization of music in educating is a methodology that licenses for this system to occur. If you blended the music while learning loads of students will have a great time and when they have a fabulous time, their psyches would be viable simultaneously, and they can think about a variety of things. That is, as of now demonstrating the viability of learning.

Quickened learning systems can exceptionally affect students whose exhibitions are truly low that varies over a wide range. This is for those students who get uninterested and lose fixation in a subject.

As a run of the mill of training, educators should continue boosting their final product of advances in capability and mind look into. It is dependent upon them to assemble critical elements of such data to their students to make their investigations alive and educated. It is dependent upon them to impart in their students' brains the significance of this data for their future. These methods are useful to develop the psyches of the youthful students to have the option to accelerate their learning and have the opportunity to get in with the world's requests.

Quickened Learning Techniques - Tips and Tricks

So you need to learn quickened learning? Perhaps you have known about it from companions, or possibly you thought that it was on the web, or hell maybe you know the vast majority of the methods and aptitudes.

This chapter is heard about attempting to support you.

So here we go! Ahead to our quickened learning methods!

1. Mental aides. Memory aids are one of the top approaches to retain anything rapidly. Become accustomed to making a relationship to recall things.

2. Utilize your faculties Want to recall the atomic structure of a particle? Need assistance remembering essential (or troublesome) words for English? This is, perhaps the ideal ways! While considering it partner it with at any rate three detects, so close your eyes and see the word, recipe, or whatever structure in your brain. Make it move around when it enters as well and include a sound. To finish it off include a smell or perhaps a splendid shading. Or on the other hand, you could do both. This system is unquestionably the best.

3. Use mind mapping I could complete an entire book on this system! What you

need to do is take Associations and memory aides to the additional level. Each time you hear, see or think something partner it with something simple to recall. At that point at whatever point you have to review something utilize the law of Association. This works superior to anything it sounds, trust me on this. I used to question it as well.

4. Focus! This is quickened learning? Here is a little thing I adapted some time in the past, to get any strategy to work you have to focus on what you are learning, all the more regularly than not our cerebrums our half sleeping. To fix this issue give denoting a slice a shot your paper each time you space out, this won't just bring you back, however, help you understand what you have to chip away at.

The Secret Habits of Highly Productive People

So how would you become highly productive?

To start with, you should guarantee that your objectives and targets are recorded as a hard copy. For every purpose and goal, it is additionally essential to list what you're attempting to achieve, alongside your inspiration driving why completing those objectives and destinations matter.

When this is finished, the subsequent stage is to make a point by point activity plan(s) for accomplishing those objectives and goals. Make sure to feature, and organize, every one of the means required, alongside including activity owner(s) and courses of events. By organizing your objectives and destinations, you'll realize where to center your time and vitality, consequently being progressively proficient, viable, and productive.

If it's not too much trouble guarantee that you comply with the time constraints that were presented, particularly for significant objectives and goals, the aim isn't to list unrealistic courses of events for accomplishing your objectives however to take into account satisfactory time to achieve every one of the undertakings recorded with the quality that it merits.

Last, and above all, is the focus. To be highly productive and useful, you should be able to focus your gifts and capacities on finishing assignments with the most noteworthy yield. Keep in mind, one of the fundamental objectives is to distribute your gifts and abilities so that you accomplish the most noteworthy conceivable profit for the vitality you put into any undertaking or task. To guarantee that your time and energy is apportioned carefully, it's ideal for concentrating and focussing on errands that take into account your qualities. The reason being is that you do things that you're great at, not exclusively will you be increasingly productive while having a fabulous time yet also commit fewer errors all the while, in this way submitting higher nature of work.

What's more, you should likewise guarantee that you center around the chances of things to come instead of tending to the issues of the past. This idea is like how fruitful associations utilize their assets - the gifts of their best individuals are distributed to the best up and coming open doors for the firm. As opposed to concentrating your vitality on a ton of unremarkable undertakings that includes no genuine worth, individuals must utilize their assets to focus on assignments that have any effect. By concentrating your endeavors on crucial territories, you'll have the option to accomplish the most critical outcomes at all measure of time.

If it's not too much trouble, note that highly productive individuals don't race through their errands. Instead, these people keep up an enduring work pace mood that enables them to finish a colossal measure of work without getting to be restless or pushed. The reason being is that highly productive individuals have figured out how to ace the craft of "center and fixation" for significant errands that will have a positive effect in accomplishing their objectives and goals throughout everyday life and they don't stop until their assignment is finished!!

Step by step instructions to Make Money and Become More Productive

A great many people would prefer only not to profit; they need to get more cash-flow. Sadly the more significant part believes that they will achieve this by working harder and more. They neglect to understand that the way to making more cash is in ending up increasingly productive. Thus the need is to work more efficiently. Here are a couple of tips that I have learned as an entrepreneur that has helped me to become increasingly productive.

Worth your time. It has been said that "time is our most valuable ware," and separated from great wellbeing I would state that this announcement is valid. We, as a whole, know the inclination when somebody demonstrates an absence of thankfulness for our time. Regularly individuals who treat others with this absence of respect don't esteem their own time either. To become progressively productive, don't waste your most valuable item and set clear limits with the goal that others will appreciate your time as much as you do.

Be great at what you do. There are the individuals who will work as long as they can remember squeezing out a living basically because they are average at what they do. Specialists are well known for this. Abstain from becoming hopelessly enamored with a lifelong way before surveying if you incline the work. Being straightforward with yourself in such a manner will pay profits. Find what you are excellent from the start, at that point figure out how to appreciate doing that.

Have an activity. One of my preferred proverbs states: "He that is watching wind won't plant." If you are trusting that the ideal minute will venture out accomplishing something, that minute is never going to come.

Be focussed and organize assignments. There is another platitude that, "if one doesn't know where they are cruising, no wind is a decent wind." I watch even fruitful individuals go around like chickens with their heads cut off. To become progressively productive one should be "coordinating their blows so as not to strike the breeze." Be focussed and organize your undertakings. Work consistently and do what should be done first, at that point proceed onward to other, less earnest projects.

Maintain a strategic distance from the diversion. Life has numerous distractions. When they show up, they separate our concentration, and our vitality begins to move to "performing multiple tasks." Even though running a heap of clothing while at the same time working from a home office may be innocuous enough, exchanging unendingly from venture to extend is undoubtedly not. Attempt to kill your telephone or check messages just at endorsed times of the day. Individuals should regard that you are a bustling individual and comprehend when you don't hit them up inside 5 minutes. When they don't understand, you would prefer not to work with them in any case.

Evade obligation. Even though a few duties might be essential, by not connecting for things before you can bear the cost of them will assist you with avoiding the weight of conveying an additional obligation load. Have you at any point attempted to push a handcart that has been heaped up excessively high? Take a gander at your budgetary way with this point of view. Indeed, you may most likely push that heap gradually, yet begin losing air in your tire and you could before long end up ceased dead, or notwithstanding rolling in reverse.

Chapter 6: Building Good Habits to Boost Your Memory

Sharpening Your Memory

Once you've organized your daily routine, you are ready to begin changing your life even further. These following recommendations are tried and tested and can help everyone, whether you are a:

·Student
·Parent
·Work full or part-time
·Company Director
·Retired
· Interested in improving your mind.

This is a guide meant for anyone who wishes to be successful in their life. All you must learn to do is use the tools of your own abilities. No financial investment is necessary, only the investment of your time.

Changes you should already have started to include in your life:

·Home cooked food
·Eliminating, or at least heavily reducing, sugars, carbs, and processed foods.

·Achieving, at the very least, the basic recommended weekly exercises.

·As a plus, if you have achieved all the above, your sleeping pattern should be much healthier.

·Finally, if stress begins to creep into your life, you should practice relaxation exercise. Breathing techniques should become a part of your life as should relaxing your muscles as I have shown you in chapter 2.

What is Memory?

The next step in achieving your goals towards accelerated learning is to improve your memory. Anyone with the right mindset and determination can improve their memory. Even those who use excuses, such as:

· My memory is poor; it'll never improve."

·I'm too old."

·I'm too busy."

· I can't be bothered."

·It's all a load of rubbish."

·I'm not clever enough."

60

Guess what - "I'm happy to announce to you that all the above are indeed nothing but poor excuses!" There is no reason why you cannot improve your memory, no matter your age or career choices. Whilst you can never achieve a photographic memory, there is much you can do to improve your day to day recall. By following our memory techniques, you will achieve the ability to focus. This will lead on to becoming more successful in your career, and in your general wellbeing.

Let's return to that powerful organ, the brain. Even more specifically, those neurons we discussed earlier. They are the brain cells and nerves that make up your brains communication network. The activity of those neurons transmits all the information that you see, smell, feel and learn in your everyday life.

Your brain decides if the new information you have absorbed is worth keeping or not. If it's worth keeping, it is then stored in your long term memory. Otherwise, it's only stored in the short term memory.

Short term means it is information to be discarded and forgotten when you no longer needed.

The memories the brain stored in the long term memory banks can be recalled if needed again. By following the same pathway of neurons used to store the memory, the information can be called back out again. This storage system doesn't work as a photograph, capturing every detail. Sometimes when a memory is recalled, it may have become a little distorted or fuzzy. That's why you cannot totally rely on memory.

Age can weaken those neurons, and hence the system doesn't always work as well as it used to. This can be repaired though because the brain is one big muscle. It's up to you to make it stronger so it will work more   efficiently.

One of the most important processes in learning new information is your memory. If you don't learn how to utilize the memory to its full potential, then it's pointless learning new things. The brain will simply assume it is useless information and only store it in the short term memory. If though, you have good memory recall, you could potentially learn a wide range of new skills. For this reason, it's important to improve your memory skills. Only then can you begin to consider accelerated learning as an exciting way forward. By developing your memory skills, you are exercising your brain to be more efficient. Exercises such as these will extend your neuron pathways. Only then can you store more knowledge, making your mind much sharper.

Mnemonics

The name of the Goddess of Memory in ancient Greek was Mnemosyne, meaning "remembrance." The ancient Greek word "mnemoniks," means "related to memory." These words have developed into the modern term of mnemonics, which is the study of improving our memory.

Mnemonics are a way of associating cues, images, sounds or abbreviations to help us remember large pieces of information. Here are some common mnemonics that

most may be familiar with: •I" before "e" except after "c." Of course, this is not 100% proof, but it's a good rule of thumb for spellings.
•Here's a good way of remembering the same word spelled two-ways but has two different meanings. "A "principal" in a school is your PAL." Whereas, a "principle" that is something you believe in, is a rule."
•A way to remember where the points are on a compass is to spell out the word "NEWS" in an "S" shape. N (North) placed at the top. E (East) placed on the left. W (West) placed on the right and opposite E. Finishing with S (South) at the bottom.

As you can see, these aren't foolproof. As well as using the common ones, you can make your own up so you can remember things better.

Billy always spelled the word "restaurant" incorrect. He wrote it down as "restarAUNT." His problem was that he confused the ending with the two ways of spelling "aunt" and "ant." It was just one of those words that confused him, as can happen to us all. To remember the right type of "aunt," or "ant," at the end of the word, he told himself that whenever he thought of eating out, he would relate it to a bug. From then onwards he knew the ending of the word was spelled as "ANT."

Mnemonics can have a broad spectrum in covering ways of association. It has proven to be successful in memory recall. You may, though, have to remember an entire poem just so you can recall something factual, such as the days of the month:

30 days hath September, April, June, and November

All the rest have 31 except for February alone.

That has 28 with an extra one in a leap year.

It's the sort of rhyme you learn as a child and carry it through to adulthood. Many adults continue to use it to recall how many days there are in a month.

Mnemonics can be much more complex than these simple examples. You can even use images, such as in this biology question you might get in an exam paper:

·Question: Name 3 depressant drugs.

·Answer: Barbiturates, Alcohol, and Tranquilizers, whereby the initials spell BAT. If you had this question in an exam, you could remind yourself to visualize a bat.

You can create mnemonics in many forms:

·Patterns of letters such as acronyms

·Short phrases

· Images

·Numbers

·Poems

·Charts

·Songs

Do you remember the ABC song you might have sung as a child so you could learn the alphabet? It is a process that can be used at any age. By learning the order of a short phrase, that phrase can then lead on to recalling the order of the planets. There's even an entire song to help you recall all 50 states in the USA. What a powerful tool Mnemonics can be.

Loci Memory Palace

There is an alternative and effective mnemonic technique to enhance your memory. It is also one of the oldest memory techniques known as the Loci Method. Some may know it as a Memory Palace, Mind Palace or even the Memory Journey. It's believed to have originated from the Roman Empire and is sometimes known as the Roman Room technique. The method uses only one room and the items within that room. Loci is a Latin word meaning "Places." That is exactly what you need when you choose to use this method. For the Loci method to be successful, you will use a familiar place that you know, such as your own home. You can use any building as long as you know the layout. To begin the Loci technique, you must imagine every aspect of your chosen location. That means the layout of the building and things such as furniture, ornaments, and pictures on the walls. This is important because each item is linked mentally to the facts you want to remember. Let's take you through a Mind Palace Journey:

· The idea is to associate something you need to memorize with a part of the building you have chosen.

· Walk through the front door, associate the first memory you want to recall with the door. Though its' not enough to simply associate the memory item with the door. Expand on this and visualize something unusual with the memory and the door. For example, if you need to remember a regular time for a train journey, then visualize a speeding train crashing through that particular door. Be imaginative as you go around your "place" associating memories with items. The more extreme the vision in your mind, the more likely you are to remember it. After all, don't we all remember the bad memories and never the good ones?

· Going on, as you step through the door, visualize the hallway. It may have a mirror and coat hooks in particular places.

· Associate more facts with each picture and each piece of furniture as you walk through rooms. You can have each room for a particular theme of memories. This is great if you're studying different subjects.

It is quite hard work and tiring and does take some time to build up your memory palace. Deep concentration implants the memory association. Then further concentration is needed to recall the information throughout your memory palace. Don't expect this to happen in a day.

It does take practice but believes in your ability to do it because it has been proven to work. Clemens Mayer won the World Memory Championship in 2006, by using a Loci Memory Palace. He had 300 stop points in a journey throughout his own home. Each stop point was a memory he needed to recall.

If you manage to get the hang of it and it works for you, there is no reason why you can't have more than one "place." Each place can consist of different sets of facts that you need to memorize. Imagine the potential for your career; it is truly mind-boggling how far you could take this method.

Chapter 7: Stop Procrastinating

Procrastination comes from the Latin words for forward (pro) and tomorrow (cras), so it literally means to push something until tomorrow. Most of us procrastinate at some point, and yet nobody sings the praises of procrastination as a learning technique.

Procrastination can cause serious problems for students. Assignments that are completed at the last minute may be sloppy and full of errors. Procrastination also causes stress and anxiety, neither of which is conducive to learning.

Key Causes of Procrastination

Let's start by talking about the key causes of procrastination. People who procrastinate are sometimes accused of laziness, but it is rarely pure laziness that causes it.

Fear of Failure/Fear of Success

It might surprise you to see fear of failure and fear of success grouped together, but it shouldn't. After all, they are flip sides of the same coin.

Students fear failure for obvious reasons, but sometimes they fear success too. They might believe that if they succeed once, they'll have to live up to a very high standard next time. Or, they might fear that they won't be able to handle harder work, which they might get if they do too well at their current level.

Identifying these fears can be hard to do, but it can be helpful to ask yourself if fear plays a role in your tendency to procrastinate.

Overwhelm

Students with a lot of work to do sometimes procrastinate because they simply don't know where to begin. Having too much work on your plate can result in a sort of brain freeze – an inability to do anything at all.

It's rare in school for teachers to confer with one another and space out assignments. Therefore, you'll have to learn to cope with juggling multiple assignments to be sure you can get everything done.

Lack of Interest

When a class doesn't interest you or seems unimportant, it can be hard to discipline yourself to get things done. Students tend to push off the assignments that they like the least – which of course only makes things harder when the time comes to get them done.

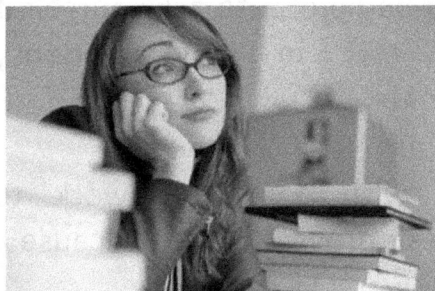

The desire to put off work you don't like is a natural one, but it's also an invitation to stress and failure. Many people find that putting unpleasant
tasks first helps them complete them – and give them energy for the tasks that remain.

What Should be on Your To-Do List

One of the things that students do that can lead to procrastination is making to-do lists that are too broad or overwhelming to be useful. For example, if you put something on your list that you know will take several days to complete, it might seem to be hanging over you in a way that feels menacing.

The key is to learn to put only tasks (simple things that can be completed in one sitting) on your to-do list. A big goal such as writing a paper or studying for an exam might break down into many small tasks. For example, to write a paper you might need to visit the library and check out books, do online research, write an outline, and so on.

Whenever you get an assignment, break it down into individual tasks. Then keep a separate to-do list for each assignment that you combine with a master list to keep you on track from day to day.

Making Tasks Meaningful

Another technique that can help you avoid procrastination is to make each task you do meaningful to you in some way. For example, you might like to be in the lab but hate writing up lab reports. You might tell yourself that the lab report needs to be written for you to be able to go to your next lab – or that having the skill to write good reports will help you land the job of your dreams.

For unwanted or unpleasant tasks, find a way to attach meaning to them – something that will motivate you to get it done.

Accountability

Finally, it's important to hold yourself accountable for what you do and don't do. Your teachers may hold you accountable, but you need to be just as accountable to yourself.

You can increase accountability by creating a study chart or by finding a study partner to hold you accountable for the time you spend working. Working with a partner or a team can really help you stay on task because you won't want to let them down.

All of these techniques and tips can help you stop procrastinating and complete your assignments on time.

Coming up next, I'll share some information about active learning and how it can help you in and out of the classroom.

Chapter 8: The Top Ten Habits of Accelerated Learners

Okay, so you now know what things you have likely been doing that are sabotaging your studying and attempts at learning. But, knowing what not to do is just halt the battle, you need to replace those bad habits with good ones to ensure you are going to effectively learn how to learn.

Again, this is not a "one–size–fits–all" kind of situation, so approach this list with an open mind, and find what works for you. That could be all that is on the list, or it might be half of the list. Just trust me, regardless of how many of these pointers you take away and apply to your own life, you are going to see a marked difference in how you are able to learn and retain the knowledge that you have learned.

So let's begin:

Don't try to get all your studying or learning done in a single session – I can't say enough how bad cramming for exams is bad for you, but it doesn't just apply to students. No matter what you are attempting to learn, even if it is just for your own pleasure, you are going to get so much more out of what you study if you spread out the topic over more than one study session.

Set aside a specific amount of time for studying – have you ever sat down to study something for a few minutes before you had to do something else or be somewhere, and you found that the entire time you were supposed to be studying you were worried that you were going to be late for your other engagement?

Instead, set aside a specific time and a specific length of time you are going to study, then truly spend that time doing what you have come there to do – study.

Study at the same time every day – routine is incredible important when it comes to studying, as with everything else you do in your day. Set up a schedule and stick to it as best as you can, ensuring that you not only study for the allotted time in a day, but that you study at the same time in a day as well.

Study with a set purpose (have a goal in mind) – when you are learning a new technique, such as a musical instrument, it is recommended that you practice with intent. This means you have a certain point in the song each day you wish to master for that session.

You can apply the same idea to studying. Set a goal for how far you wish to reach that day, then study until you get there.

Don't procrastinate with your study session – when you put things off, you just set up in your mind how little you want to do them, then when you finally do get around to it, you rush and you get sloppy with the results.

Treat your learning with respect, and when you attempt to learn new material, prioritize it in your day as much as possible. View it as a positive thing that you want to do, and you are going to find that it not only isn't as bad as you think it's going be, but you are going to learn much faster than you do when you simply fit it in around the cracks.

Study the hardest part of what you need to learn firsts – there is always going to be some part of the material that you really don't want to do, so be responsible there, too, and get it out of the way while your brain is ready to focus and get things done. Once you are done with the hardest part, the rest of the work isn't going to seem as bad anyway, which will, in turn, make your entire session go a lot better than you thought it was going to.

Take notes throughout your study, and don't be afraid to review them – remember what I said about note taking? Yes, it's that important. Don't neglect to jot down this or that when you are studying, and keep your notes organized so you can refer back to them quickly when you need to. A good note taker knows when and how to use the notes to their advantage, and you will, too.

Get rid of distractions – distractions are different for everyone, and they come in all shapes and forms. You might think you are hungry or thirsty, when really you are looking for a way to get out of what you are doing. You might find listening to music helps, you might find that it's the worst thing you can do.

Know yourself well enough to know what kind of distractions get to you the most, and do your part in avoiding them. It's an extra step in the beginning, but it is going to pay off in the end, trust me.

Find a support system of any kind – this doesn't even need to be a physical support system. Just find somewhere you can go where you are going to be motivated to study – perhaps a coffees shop, a park, a library, or wherever. As long as you get there and you feel like you can stick with your studies, you are in good company.

As I said, learning is a very personal journey, and you are going to have to find what works best for you. These nine tips are sure to impact your study session, but you must not forget tip number ten:

Practice makes perfect. If you are a student, don't allow yourself to forget about school when you aren't currently in the classroom. Instead, take a few minutes in the evening and on the weekends to do a quick review of the material you have taken note of. It's not going to take you long to look over during this time, and it's going to make a world of difference when you are finally tested on the material.

At the same time, if you are an adult and you are attempting to learn something quickly for your job, an upcoming event, or whatever the situation may be, glance over your notes when you are making dinner, or after you have settled down for the evening. Again, it doesn't take long for you to do, but it makes all the difference in your final outcome.

CHAPTER 9: Practical Speed Reading Techniques to Help You Read Faster

Alright, let's now get into serious business. First of all, speed reading is not rocket science. I say this because many people seem to be intimidated by the concept. They think of speed reading as a very complicated skill that only the super talented can learn. This is absolutely not the case at all. Anyone can develop the skill of speed reading. To learn how to do it, all you need is time and patience. In fact, you might already be using some of the techniques discussed below. You are just not aware that it constitutes speed reading. Anyway, let's dig in now, shall we?

1. The Pointer Method

- As the term implies, this method involves pointing at the words, sentences, and paragraphs that you are reading. This method is also sometimes referred to as "hand pacing" or "meta guiding". It basically involves sweeping your finger along the line as you read. You can also use a card instead of your finger. Just slowly bring the card down each line as you read through the sentences. This is one of the preferred methods of Evelyn Nielsen Wood, the woman who first popularized the concept of speed reading.

2. The Tracker and Pacer Method

- This is actually a variant of the pointer method. Instead of using your finger or a card, use a pen with its cap still on. As you read through a sentence, keep the pen just below the words you are reading. Move the tip of the pen forward as you read. Your eyes should be focused just above the tip of the pen. Practitioners of this method suggest that you should try not to spend more than one second with each line. Majority of the people who try this method for the first time retain very little information from what they are reading. This is okay and it's completely normal. Just like any skill, speed reading is something that you learn over time. With that said, if you want to master the tracker and pacer method, you must practice as often as you can.

3. The Scanning or Previewing Method
- This is a method that's very difficult to master but it's one of the most effective and efficient. If you are able to master this method, you can read and understand the context of whole paragraphs in just mere seconds. The method involves using your eyes to quickly scan through the page. You start from the top of the page and move quickly down to the center, to the bottom of the page, then scan back up the page. As you scan through the page, you start identifying and registering specific words and phrases that are crucial to understanding the context of the paragraphs. These can be small phrases, whole sentences, numbers, names, dates, and other types of trigger words.

For sure, you are not going to read every single word in the text, but you are going to get its context. Your eyes will land on the information that matters and that's the important part. This is especially true in reading non-fiction types of content wherein you don't need to savor every word or every sentence. To get the most out of this method, you need to expand your peripheral vision. Train your eyes to quickly scan the page and determine what's important and what's not.

In short, scanning is a process of actively looking for information in a wall of text using a mind- map. To create the mind-map, organize the information you are looking at in a visually hierarchical manner. Such a visual hierarchy should showcase the interrelatedness of the words, sentences, and paragraphs. With a mind- map, it is much easier to retrieve and understand the information you are trying to process.

4. The Skimming Method

- With this technique, quickly skim through the sentences in a page for an attempt to find clues to the main topic or idea. You instantly make a list of these clues in your mind, put them all together, and try to understand what the page is all about. The skimming method is most commonly employed when reading essays that you want to read as quickly as possible. Skimming can mean reading the beginning sentences or ending sentences for summary information then going back to read for further details. This easily cuts off the number of minutes you need to read the whole essay.

Of course, the skimming method is not perfect just like most of the speed reading techniques discussed in this book. It can have a significant effect on your comprehension. There is always the possibility that you miss out on important details and information in a page and you end up getting the wrong context or the wrong ideas. But as far as increasing your speed reading time is concerned, skimming is as powerful as they come.

With practice, you can increase your reading speed to seven hundred (700) words per minute which is way beyond the normal two hundred (200) to three hundred (300) words per minute. Skimming is best implemented when reading short articles. You can read through the headings and beginning sentences and you will soon get an idea of what the articles are about.

5. Rapid Serial Visual Presentation (RSVP) Method

- This is a fairly new method because it is mostly utilized by the digital speed reading systems that have recently popped up in the market. Single words or phrases would flash out on the screen of your device so that you are concentrating on a single word or phrase at a time. The more you get used to the system, the more you learn how to speed up the display of words and phrases.

Today, there are several apps that use this method to help people with their speed reading skills. Such apps include Spreed, Open Spritz, Syllable, Velocity, and Outread. You should consider checking these out and exploring which app best suits you. They have helped thousands of people read faster. They might be able to help you as well.

6. The Perceptual Expansion Technique

- It has been scientifically discovered that if you train your peripheral vision to register words more effectively, you can significantly increase your reading speed up to over 300%. Yes, up to 300%. That means if your normal reading speed is 25o words per minute, you can increase it up to 750 words per minute using the perceptual expansion technique.

Here's how it works: If you focus your attention on the center of a page, you will realize that you can still see the outer edges of the page. Untrained readers would usually use one-half of their peripheral vision on margins by reading from the first word to the last word on a line on a page. This means that they are spending 25% to 50% of their time reading margins with zero content. Needless to say, this is a major waste of time.

This is where the perceptual expansion technique comes to work. You would have to widen your peripheral vision so you don't have to constantly move left to right from margin to margin. The only thing you should be moving are your eyes. And this is if you are reading a large book or if you are looking at a huge computer screen. But if you are reading a small pocket book, then there's even no need to move your eyes that much. With the perceptual expansion technique, you can widen your vision so that you can focus on everything without wasting your time on a page.

7. The Page-Turning Technique

- I know that some of you are going to find this technique trivial or even absurd but allow me to convince you why it's important and why it matters. The page-turning technique is very simple. Just turn the page as quickly as you can to save time. Simply put, it will only take you one second or less to turn the page in a book. However, studies show that majority of people spend more than one second to turn a book. Let's say that it takes you three seconds to turn the page in a book instead of just one second. There's a difference of two seconds. If that book is five hundred (500) pages long, that means you wasted around 1000 seconds just turning the pages. That is a total of seventeen (17) minutes wasted. The extra two seconds you spend turning a page may not look much but they are significant when they accumulate.

Needless to say, you need to turn the pages as fast as you can. The best way to do this is to get ready to turn the page when you are near the last lines in a page. You don't have to read to the last word before you turn the page. You can turn the page as you read the last sentence. This is very easy to do for most readers. Some of us just developed the habit of taking forever to turn the page. Get rid of that habit and you can substantially increase the number of pages you can read in less time.

8. The Skipping or Selective Reading Strategy

- With this method, you simply skip reading an entire section altogether. There are two main reasons why you should skip reading a certain section in a page. One, there is nothing new in the material. And two, the section doesn't cover a topic that you need to know. In short, the skipping method involves spotting content that are unnecessary or merely fillers. This is why skipping is sometimes referred to as the selective reading technique. You select what you need to read and ignore the rest. Skipping is most effective when you are reading through content that you are very familiar with. For example, you are a fan of the sport of soccer and you are reading a news article about the latest developments in the sport. You don't have to read the whole article because you already know most of it. Just skip to the pieces of information that you don't know about.

9. The Under Pressure Technique

- In many ways, this method is a time management strategy. What you do is give yourself a specific window of time to read a page or an article. For example, let's say that you have a 200-page book that you must read quickly in preparation for a book report. You need to finish your report because the deadline is approaching. To make sure that you finish reading the book on time, you decide to read each page for just 30 seconds. Doing the math, you are going to finish the book in 100 minutes or one hour and 40 minutes. This is why this method is called the under pressure technique. You are pressuring yourself to finish reading a book or an article in a short period of time. This method can be very difficult at first. Let's be honest here; reading a page in just 30 minutes seems unattainable and unsustainable. But just like any skill, it can be done with regular practice. The trick to mastering this technique is to combine it with some of the speed reading techniques discussed in this book. For instance, you can use the under pressure technique with the scanning and skimming methods.

10. Focus on the Headings

- Just by looking at the headings in an article or in a book, you can quickly get an idea of what the succeeding paragraphs would be about. In some instances, you can just read the headings and you can get the whole gist of the page. Headings are like the seeds from which ideas put forth in the article or book sprout from. Focusing on headings is very important especially in the digital age. If you regularly read online articles, then you know how heavy these are when it comes to headings.

After quickly scanning through the headings, only then do you decide if it's worth reading the entirety of the paragraphs. Writers are usually trained to guide their readers by packing as much information as possible in their headings. This plays well to your advantage because you get to glean more details just by looking at the headings.

The main takeaway you should get from this chapter is that there are nearly a dozen ways on how you can improve your speed reading capabilities. Speed reading is a skill and just like any type of skill, you get better at it with practice and constant implementation. The more you use any of the techniques and strategies discussed above, the more efficient you become with your reading and comprehension skills. You may have noticed by now that all of the methods mentioned here can't stand on their own. What I mean by this is that you often have to use two or more of them at the same time to get the maximum effect. For example, you can get the most out of the skipping method by combining it with the tracker and pacer technique.

I am not in any way saying that you should use every single one of these speed reading techniques. That would be next to impossible if I'm going to be honest about it. However, I would highly recommend that you at least try all of them to see which methods will generate the best results for you. There's no such thing as "the best speed reading technique". What's best for you may be the worst method for someone else. This is why I'm recommending that you take the time to try all the methods for you to be able to determine which ones you are going to use.

Chapter 10: Learn by practice

The practice is significant for educating and learning in at any rate five different ways: Practice extraordinarily improves the probability that understudies will forever recollect new data. When understudies work on taking care of issues, they increment their capacity to move rehearsed aptitudes to new and progressively complex issues

Distributed practice, otherwise called dispersed practice, is a procedure of discovering that utilizes littler additions of study and practice over a more drawn out timeframe as opposed to "massed work on". In a scholarly situation, this is the distinction between utilizing quality investigation time day by day to get familiar with a subject as opposed to "packing" directly before a test. The dispersed practice has been demonstrated to be more compelling for learning and memory maintenance than massed practice.

4.1 Distributed practice

Distributed practice is a system whereby the understudy appropriates his/her examination exertion in a given course over many investigation sessions that are moderately short in a span. This can be contrasted with massed practice (also called packing) whereby the understudy conducts not many however long investigation sessions for a given course. It has been demonstrated without question that important learning is advanced when the dispersed practice is led. Interestingly, massed practice advances repetition learning. For the long haul advantage of the understudy, circulated practice ought to be the strategy a superb understudy decides to utilize. Following a 4-multi year school vocation, an understudy who pursued the disseminated practice method would be miles in front of an understudy who pursued the massed practice strategy. Lamentably, some school courses energize massed practice by giving just 2-3 tests during the semester (and little else for evaluation). At the point when just 2-3 tests are given, the understudy masses study sessions quickly preceding every test. This testing recurrence (2-3 tests/semester) likewise advances, the less alluring, repetition learning.

In what capacity can an understudy actualize Distributed practice? All things considered, it takes inspiration and assurance to get this show on the road. Likely one great path is to plan study times on seven days to week premise toward the start of every semester. That is, put aside one brief examination session every day for each course. Do this for Monday through Saturday, leaving Sunday as an offday or make up for lost time day or even as an all-out unwinding day or family day. After the semester gets this show on the road, changes may be finished. Maybe a few courses needn't bother with the every day brief examination session M-Sat. with certain sessions skipped during the week. In different cases, a few courses may require more than one everyday study session. Just the individual understudy can pass judgment on whether changes are required. On the off chance that an understudy needs so much investigation time that there isn't sufficient time in the day to plan sessions, that understudy ought to think about dropping a course or two.

For the Distributed practice to be effective, the understudy must have the option to pursue his/her investigation plan. Try not to let interferences ruin it. Think about your investigation plan as a work routine, something that must be pursued. On the off chance that you locate that others/different exercises keep you from keeping on a plan, at that point you are going to flounder. Go cover-up somewhere during your examination sessions (the library works useful for this in the event that you discover a corner up in the stacks). Another indication, take study breaks-study for 50 minutes at that point get up for a 5 brief break. At that point return to business as a usual subject, or even better, go on to another subject. Another insight makes an effort not to take two comparative courses during a similar semester. Some of the time when an understudy takes two comparative courses, material from one class may meddle with the capacity to learn the material in a different class. This isn't generally the situation, however when all is said in done it is smarter to take courses (in any one semester) that are unmistakable from one another.

4.2 Retrieval practice

Retrieval practice is a system wherein carrying data to mind upgrades and lifts learning. Intentionally reviewing data compels us to pull our insight "out" and look at what we know.

For example, reviewing a response to a science question improves figuring out how to a more prominent degree than looking into the appropriate response in a course reading. Also, having to really review and record a response to a cheat sheet improves adapting more than believing that you know the appropriate response and flipping the card over rashly.

Regularly, we think we've adapted some snippet of data, however, we come to acknowledge we battle when we attempt to review the appropriate response. It's definitely this "battle" or challenge that improves our memory and learning – by attempting to review data, we practice or fortify our memory, and we can likewise recognize holes in our learning.

Note that psychological researchers used to allude to recovery practice as "the testing impact." Prior research inspected the intriguing finding that tests (or short tests) drastically improve learning. All the more as of late, scientists have exhibited that more than essentially tests and tests improve learning: cheat sheets, practice issues, composing prompts, and so forth are additionally integral assets for improving learning.

Regardless of whether this incredible system is called Retrieval practice or the testing impact, it is essential to remember that the demonstration of pulling data "out" from our brains significantly improves learning, not simply the tests. As it were Retrieval is the dynamic procedure we participate in to support learning; tests and tests are just strategies to advance recovery.

Retrieval practice makes learning effortful and testing. Since recovering data requires mental exertion, we regularly think we are doing ineffectively in the event that we can't recall something. We may feel like advancement is moderate, however, that is the point at which our best learning happens. The more troublesome the recovery practice, the better it is for long haul learning.

Attempting to learn – through the demonstration of rehearsing what you know and reviewing data – is considerably more viable than re-perusing, taking notes, or tuning in to addresses. More slow, effortful recovery prompts long haul learning. Conversely, quick, simple techniques just lead to momentary learning.

Retrieval Practice in the Workplace

In the realm of grown-up learning, there are numerous occupations that require recalling immense measures of data. Recovery based learning could be a compelling procedure. For instance, consider all the activity jobs that include snappy basic leadership, when there isn't a great opportunity to look for outer help. Likewise, consider every one of the jobs where there is essentially no methods for outer help with the goal that the individual must remember everything.

Here are a few procedures that learning experience originators can use to encourage Retrieval based learning.

☐ Improve metacognition. Numerous individuals anticipate that on the off chance that they basically re-study material it will expand maintenance. This isn't the best approach. Assist students with seeing that a progressively powerful technique for upgrading learning and long haul maintenance is to over and again work on reviewing the data one has considered (Karpicke, 2012).

☐ Practice with certifiabe situations. Studies show the significance of setting in recovery. At the point when members over and again recover information in a testing domain, they perform better on the test. On the off chance that the setting of learning influences how we recreate information, at that point rehearsing recovery in a wide scope of reenactments will presumably have a comparative impact.

☐ Give different self-checks and activities. Since rehashed review increments long haul maintenance, give various chances to students to test themselves for basic data. You may need to educate students about the adequacy regarding recovery based figuring out how to rouse them to finish a subsequent self-check.

☐ Separated Retrieval practice. Dividing the recovery practice after some time is more viable than massed recovery practice.

☐ Give chances to assemble talks. After a learning occasion, exploit discourses (either on the web or face to face) that encourage the review of basic information. Do this with centered addressing.

Best Strategy for Long-term Retention

The customary way to deal with long haul realizing, which requires an individual to review and utilize information, is rehashed study. Be that as it may, concentrating a similar data again and again (known as a massed study) has its points of confinement. Luckily, there is an increasingly proficient methodology.

Steady research shows that the missing fixing to many investigation schedules is practice with recovery otherwise called the testing impact (Karpicke, 2012). The rehashed practice of reviewing data is an increasingly powerful learning technique for long haul maintenance than rehashed study. This doesn't imply that contemplating is irrelevant, it implies that rehashed examination isn't as viable as rehashed recovery practice. (Tune in to my meeting with a recovery practice scientist or download the transcript.)

Encoding versus Retrieval

Only a little foundation first. The psychological hypothesis separates between two procedures of human memory: encoding and recovery. Encoding is the way toward putting away data in long haul memory and recovery is the way toward getting too learned data. Recovery is incited by a recovery signal, which is a question, understanding or occasion that initiates related information.

Significance of the Retrieval Cue

Recovery signals are significant in light of the fact that they are the key that opens the data. Envision a recently graduated class of firemen. They all breezed through the assessment, however, what number of them will have the option to review the particular information required to deal with a special circumstance? Just the individuals who have the suitably adjusted recovery prompts accessible can recoup the vital data.

Is it actually that basic?

All things considered, no. Recovery isn't exactly that basic. In his article, Retrievalbased Learning, partner teacher Jeffrey Karpicke states, "Individuals don't store static, precise of encounters that are replicated verbatim at recovery. Rather, information is effectively remade based on the present setting and accessible recovery signs."

4.3 Deliberate Practice

Deliberate practice alludes to an exceptional sort of training that is deliberate and methodical. While the standard practice may incorporate thoughtless redundancies, Deliberate practice requires centered consideration and is directed with the particular objective of improving execution.

Conscious practice doesn't imply that you can design yourself into anything with enough work and exertion, however. While people do have a momentous capacity to build up their aptitudes, there are breaking points to how far any individual can go. Your qualities set a limit around what is conceivable.

Be that as it may, while hereditary qualities impact execution, they don't decide execution. Try not to mistake predetermination for circumstance. Qualities give opportunity. They don't decide our fate. It's like a round of cards. You have a superior chance in the event that you have managed a superior hand, yet you additionally need to play the hand well to win.

Notwithstanding where we decide to put forth a concentrated effort, purposeful practice can assist us with boosting our latent capacity—regardless of what cards we were managed. It transforms potential into the real world.

Deliberate practice in 6 stages
1. Get spurred

Like most beneficial interests, creating capability in any ability — in the case of sewing, programming plan, or surfing — isn't simple. On the off chance that you need to push past the hard pieces of aptitudes development — the disappointment, the disappointments, the times of moderate advancement — you're going to should be spurred.

We found in the prologue to this arrangement how one of Ericsson's first examinations in Deliberate practice depended on inspiration. Ericsson was working with an undergrad understudy to test the impact of training on transient memory. The understudy, Steve, started to improve with training until he hit a stopping point — he had arrived at the common roof of his capacities and was persuaded he couldn't go any more remote. It was Steve's focused nature and assurance to improve that roused him to continue having a go at, helping him get through to arrive at record-breaking execution in transient memory works out.

Without the inspiration to push past hindrances, when improvement slows down, the regular tendency will be to surrender. So in case, you're picking expertise to improve with Deliberate practice, ensure it's something you care about and are eager to dedicate impressive time and exertion to.

2. Set explicit, practical objectives

Inspiration additionally requires keeping your focus on the awesome end goal. What're more, obscure goals like "showing signs of improvement" at a specific aptitude won't cut it. Conventional objectives for development don't give you the inspiration to exceed expectations past your present capacities or assist you with estimating your advancement.

Deliberate practice depends on little, feasible, well-characterized steps that assist you with working your way towards significant improvement. These means should consider your present information and expertise level and drive those limits gradually, reliably growing your capacities.

3. Break out of your customary range of familiarity

For objectives to prod improvement, they have to continually challenge your present capacities. Just rehashing aptitudes you definitely realize how to do — an ineffective cycle that is anything but difficult to stall out in with customary ways to deal with training — won't really upgrade your expertise level or improve execution.

Extending yourself is the way to development. In any case, Ericsson underscores that with regards to abilities advancement, breaking out of your usual range of familiarity isn't tied in with "investing more energy" Your objectives should waver on the edge of what you are and aren't able to do. On the off chance that you can't push ahead with one system or approach, attempt another and continue testing until you get through the obstruction that is hindering your way to progress.

4. Be steady and persevering

This sort of delayed exertion will be disappointing and awkward on occasion. In any case, pushing through those predicaments frequently prompts huge improvement. One of the fundamental parts of purposeful practice — what makes it so compelling — is its normality.

In the exploration paper "The Role of Deliberate Practice in the Acquisition of Expert Performance," Ericsson and his associates share their disclosure that top entertainers, regardless of their specialized topic, kept a comparable practice routine: a brief (however extreme), day by day or semi-week by week solo practice sessions.

One of Ericsson's investigations followed grown-up musician learning at worldclass music foundations and found that the performers arrived at the midpoint of coordinated and-a-half hours daily of high-power solo practice. The investigation found that the amassed measure of this standard centered practice directly affected the artists' degree of execution.

These steady, extraordinary eruptions of exertion are vital to keeping up energy in building mastery.

Exertion of intentional practice to keep away from mental or physical weariness.

5. Look for input

"Without input," Ericsson says, "either from yourself or from outside spectators — you can't make sense of what you have to enhance or that you are so near accomplishing your objectives."

Criticism is basic for distinguishing zones for development and increasing a sensible perspective on your advancement. Regardless of whether one-on-one training with an instructor, guide or friend or some type of self-appraisal, you need a method for pinpointing your qualities and shortcomings. This is the best way to recognize and work through inconvenience spots and advance from "only all right" to genuine dominance of expertise.

6. Set aside some effort to recoup

Since purposeful practice requires your complete consideration, with maximal mental as well as physical exertion, it must be continued for a brief timeframe. Research center investigations of expanded practice have topped the ideal time at one hour out of each day, three to five days per week, and genuine examinations have seen decreased advantages when practice sessions surpass two hours.

This degree of power and focus make recuperation time significant. Ericsson has seen that a significant number of the top entertainers he considered profited by snoozing. Whatever sort of recreation action or unwinding you pick, it's critical to balance the extraordinary exertion of purposeful practice to maintain a strategic distance from mental or physical weakness.

Chapter 11: HOW TO STAY FOCUSED WHILE LEARNING

Unpredictable and seemingly invincible - lack of concentration is one of our biggest enemies in everyday life. It can be prevented by simple exercises and tips and the concentration can be quickly rebuilt.

Just when you need them most, our concentration wanes. After a span of 30-90 minutes, this process becomes autonomous, as consistent focusing means great effort for the human brain. When cognitive performance is exceeded, content can no longer be successfully captured and we are looking for new stimuli that are less exhausting for us. These uncontrollable phases of distraction make sure that no more productive phase can arise.

To counter this, deliberate exercises and tips that help increase productivity can be helpful.

For almost everything, there are tools that can help us increase our performance. So also with the concentration: exercises and different tricks can help here. Because before you make a learning material, a new hobby, or even just painting a sandwich, you should first be able to concentrate on the matter . After all, most of the time your consciousness passes by and soon your bread lies on the floor with the butter side. Or you sit for hours in vain in front of the book and in the end have learned nothing about it. Now you're probably wondering how to focus at the touch of a button ? Or are you still thinking about sandwiches? In any case, you should focus briefly, then you can do it even better in the future!

Summary

Your brain is trying to save energy , so it's hard to be permanently concentrated. You can train it with mindfulness. Regular exercise and proper nutrition help concentration - exercises as well. If you need concentration quickly , banish all distractions. You eliminate annoying noises with headphones and your smartphone is best placed far away. Distracting thoughts can be temporarily switched off with meditation or a mental "worry box". Also, it can help to think in a diving bell deep under the sea, where nothing exists except you and your learning object. Still take breaks in betweenin which you hear music or move something, so that the concentration does not relax.

Your problem

It's hard to concentrate, and if you can do it, it will not be for a long time. Your thoughts are constantly wandering around rather than sticking to your task. Noises and devices (like your smartphone) are constantly distracting you.

Your solution

You can use exercises to increase concentration. These increase your focus in the longer term. There are also tools for quick application that can help you concentrate better. This allows you to specifically turn to a task and get it done.

The tool

You've probably already experienced that you do something and seconds later had no idea what just happened. Mostly it happens when reading, if you read entire paragraphs without hindsight even a word to be able to play. How is it that your brain is working so badly?

It does not, on the contrary: your brain is always trying to simplify and automate . After all, the light bulb, which appears with a good idea over your head is anything but an energy-saving lamp - more a floodlight system. Meaning, the energy consumption of our brain is so high that it was formerly vital to reduce this something. This is no longer necessary today, but it does not happen that fast. So we have to use tools to increase concentration .

4 exercises for a better concentration

Color Mandalas

The classic has been revived and has even become a trend. Mandalas are no longer just fun for kids. Special, more sophisticated adult mandalas help to relax and train the ability to concentrate. Like a fantasy journey that inspires the soul, Mandala's mind and body are also ridding themselves of mental confusion. These concrete visualizations have a meditative effect and bring the thoughts back into balance. They thus also help with acute lack of concentration, for example in the middle of a learning marathon.

Motor exercises

Exercise not only increases brain development in children, it also revives concentration. If the focus fades noticeably, a break should be taken. Here, even small motor exercises are enough to boost cognitive performance. It is often enough to walk around in the apartment, to change your sitting position or to do short fitness exercises. To start the day in a concentrated and stimulating way, you can just take a morning walk. This should be repeated several times a day with persistent lack of concentration.

Breathing exercises and meditation

When the eyes slowly get tired and the head just does not want to absorb anything, the conscious control of the breath can do wonders. It should set a fixed period of, for example, ten minutes, in which, instead of letting his mind wander again towards stress, should simply count. One breath per breath and escape from everyday life is guaranteed. This exercise has a very similar function to coloring mandalas.

Riddles and other exercises

There are also various playful methods to practice a better ability to concentrate . The regular and successful solving of riddles conditions the brain so that it can remain focused over a longer period of time. The board games "Mikado" or "Jenga" are especially helpful here.

Mental exercises that train a conscious focus, for example, when the daily routine is gone backwards again. The same effect has the reverse spelling. When you're on the go, it's enough to just follow the second hand on a watch for a long time and count the seconds. Also counting steps on the next walk is a good workout to stay focused longer while learning.

Another rich method is concentrated scripting. For this purpose, certain letters can be marked and counted in a newspaper article. Writing down words or whole sentences backwards or inverse is also helpful.

9 tips for more focus

The well-being of the body

Of course, there should be a chocolate bar here and there as a reward, but in general an optimized concentration basis can only be achieved through a vitamin-rich diet and plenty of hydration, which provide the brain with sufficient nutrients and oxygen. Sugary foods have a tiring effect. Nuts, on the other hand, provide the body with important, performance-enhancing omega-3 fatty acids. In addition, between six and seven hours of sleep is enough to stay focused. Too much sleep causes the opposite.

Variation against boredom

Even monotonous work is tedious and brings concentration weakness even faster to light. In order to rob the works of their drowsy function, variety should be brought into play. In school and study, the topics should be varied or learned in parallel for two subjects. The motivation and therefore the focus dwindle as soon as robotic and dispassionately learned. For example, an office job should switch between presentations, writing and telephone work.

Change of location are invigorating

Although it sounds extremely simple, our environment has a significant impact on our ability to concentrate. First and foremost, a place should be chosen where one feels comfortable. Bald rooms without decoration or sensual stimulation offer little potential here. In contrast, working in nature often has a very inspiring effect on us. Daylight also has an invigorating effect. If there is no direct possibility to work outside, only the space can be changed. From the study over the living room to the bedroom to the kitchen, balcony or garden should be changed again and again.

Learning in groups

This approach is certainly not for everyone, but for many people, learning in groups helps them stay focused. They feel pressurized when the others are busy next to them and they do not produce anything productive. In addition, common breaks can be inserted, which one can look forward to. It is important not to constantly digress from the topic. However, questions should not be left out altogether, because speaking together on a topic often brings many new ideas to light and helps the learner to save the material. Social contact should be built into each multi-day learning phase, as it stimulates key regions of the brain that serve to collect information.

Chapter 12: The Pareto and Pomodoro Strategies

In this chapter, you will learn two advanced strategies that can help you learn tough subjects at ease: the Pareto Principle and Pomodoro Technique.

Pareto Principle

The Pareto Principle, also known as the 80/20 rule argues that 20% of the effort should yield 80%. This principle could be used to different subjects and disciplines that you want to learn, ranging from business to literature to mathematics to engineering, and more.

This principle was introduced by a man named Joseph Juran who was inspired by the Italian economist Vilfredo Pareto (hence the name). Pareto discovered that in 1906, almost 80% of the land in Italy are owned by only 20% of the Italian population. He also discovered that 20% of the pea pods yielded 80% of the total peas.

Using the 80/20 rule or the Pareto Principle could highly affect your ability to learn. For discussion purposes, let's take language learning as an example. Using this for the acquisition of new knowledge, you should consider that the words chosen to concentrate on learning and using are the core tasks. For example, focusing your learning the top 100 most commonly used French words will produce a maximum increase in your French fluency. Focusing on the basics is crucial because you may not have the goa to acquire an exhaustive vocabulary or comprehensive mastery of the French grammar to learn how to write and speak in French.

The language and vocabulary that you choose to concentrate on studying when you want to learn a language should be a material that you would use in your own language. There are times that language learning concentrates on unclear content with the goal of promoting cultural understanding. Rather, language training must be used as a tool to explore a personal interest or discipline. In addition, most people easily give up on studying a foreign language once the lessons become boring or tedious.

In order to make the learning of language more relevant, you should think of your purpose of why you are learning the language. This is a crucial one. Studying classical French and reading old French novels will not be useful if you need to work in Paris as an engineer.

It is also a good time to spend the fundamentals of grammar of a certain language. Language training, which concentrate too much on vocabulary alone is not useful for students who want to be fluent. Once you learn the basic grammar you should practice the language by engaging in actual conversations. Covering the fundamental knowledge of the 20% of the language (grammar) can help you dominate the remaining 80% of the language use (conversation).

Pomodoro Technique

The Pomodoro Technique was developed by the Italian Francesco Cirillo in early 1980s. He utilized a kitchen timer shaped like a tomato (pomodoro in Italian) to guide anyone in chunking down tasks in 25-minute work intervals or pomodoros. This technique is founded on the theory that frequent breaks can improve the mental agility, which is crucial for the learning process.

How to Use the Pomodoro Technique

Follow the five steps below to effectively use the Pomodoro Technique:

Choose the learning activity you want to do (write an essay, read a book chapter, etc.)

Set the Pomodoro timer to 25 mins.

Pour all your effort and mental energy to do the task until the Pomodoro stops

Break for at least five minutes

Set the timer again, and work until you have completed four pomodoros. If you are not yet done, resume to work and break for 5 minutes in between.

Make certain to take note once you complete a pomodoro chunk. With this, you can develop your peace of mind and you will also develop the nice feeling of accomplishing things. Using this strategy, you can easily learn how to determine tasks that are urgent to be completed, work in a less stern setting, and chunk a large task or a project in smaller yet doable parts.

Exercises

Always use the Pareto Principle when you are learning difficult subjects. Many people find it helpful to print out a large sign containing the words "Remember, 80/20" and posting it on their work area. Through this, they are constantly reminded to use the rule.

You may need to buy a pomodoro timer, a pen, and a small notebook where you can use to record your progress. There are also special apps and program that makes it easy to use the Pomodoro Technique.

Chapter 13: Your Memory

Have you ever been at the grocery store and you forget half of the things that you came for because it slipped your busy mind to actually make a shopping list? It happens to the best—and the worst—of us.

There are so many upsides to remembering everything that you need to and so many disadvantages to forgetting everything! So let's see if we can find some ways to forget about the disadvantages and embrace the advantages of having a superb memory.

So there are a few quick fixes that you can use to help you improve your memory. The first one I want to talk about is getting sleep. If you are not getting enough sleep, and you are always tired, your brain is just not going to function as well as it could be. The best way to improve more than just your memory like your ability to understand new concepts, you should make sure that you are getting at least nine hours of sleep every single night (for adults). If you are in your late teens or early twenty's you should aim for as much as nine to 12 hours of sleep every night.

Everyone knows that exercise is an amazing thing that you could do for your body in terms of health. But did you know that it could also help improve your memory drastically? Jogging, running, or biking are all activities that you can do for just 20 to 30 minutes a few times a week in order to remember things better. There is a part of the brain called the hippocampus which is very important for your memory. When you exercise, you get your blood starts flowing to your brain and through the hippocampus, enlarging it and your memory bank.

Eating healthy is something else that you can do. This is starting to sound like a diet book, isn't it?

It's true, though! Providing the right foods and fuel for your brain is something that you can never go wrong in. Just because you eat healthy to stay energized and lean, your brain needs good fuel, too! Many foods like fish, blueberries, broccoli, and dark chocolate have all been proven to help improve memory and help you advance your brain function.

Meditation can also help you with your memory. Studies have shown that focus and concentration can enhance your memory abilities—all things that meditation encourages. When you meditate, you are simply clearing your mind and concentrating on anything else but what is happening in your everyday life. The goal is to relax your mind and body and get your mind off things.

Drinking water has also been something that has helped a lot of people who have memory problems. It may seem a little weird because water is just water. Sure it is great for your body and digestion, but how is it good for your brain? Well, your brain is a whole 73% water, meaning that being hydrated is very important.

Before we move on to some accelerated learning techniques that can help you with memory, I have one more thing that you should check out. I advise you to have a look at any medications that you are taking. Many people do not know that some medications can have negative effects on your memory and can cause you to forget things that you have remembered forever.

So how can you improve your memory through accelerated learning? Well, the best answer that I and the Internet can give you is brain games!

Playing games that improve brain function and doing brain teasers is just like doing a crazy workout for your brain. There are many games that you can play that can stretch and exercise your brain and sparkle up your memory. Some of these games that you can do include crosswords, jigsaw puzzles, chess, and Sudoku puzzles. It is important that you do not do these puzzles too often, though. If you do, you will train other parts of your brain and not so much your memory bank.

Chapter 14: Translate Newly Learned Material into Your Own Words

A method of learning that is highly effective is that of translating newly learned material into your own words. This is something that most people do not take the time to do, and the irony is that if they would they could spare themselves the copious amount of time it takes to memorize someone else's words. One of the problems with learning someone else's words is that you are essentially trying to learn their thoughts. After all, language is simply the method by which we express our thoughts for others to see, hear and understand. Therefore, when you simply try to memorize material as it is then you skip a vital element of the learning process—turning the material into your own thoughts. The difference between trying to master someone else's thoughts as opposed to forming your own is the difference between night and day in terms of learning any subject matter.

One method of translating newly learned material into your own words is to simply paraphrase the material. Large portions of written material can often prove unnecessary with regard to the subject being studied. Depending on the nature of the material itself, upward of sixty percent of the actual writing can be grammatical in nature, containing no real value in terms of the presented information itself. Therefore, paraphrasing written materials into your own words can significantly shorten the amount of material you need to refer to, thereby making studying easier and more efficient. Additionally, when you translate material into your own words your notes will become easier for you to read as they are in your natural tone and mindset. Rather than having to read and reread lofty or complicated words you can simply read your own version of the information, making it easier to comprehend.

Another way that translating newly learned information into your own words is beneficial is that it causes you to approach the material from a creative standpoint. The problem with simply memorizing information is that it only utilizes a portion of your brain. The fact of the matter is that the brain is compartmentalized, meaning that different parts of your brain perform different functions. Thus, if you rely on only one part of your brain for retaining and remembering information, then you are reducing yourself to a small percentage of your overall mental capacity. Alternatively, if you engage the creative side of your brain by rewriting material in your own words then you absorb that material in another portion of your brain, increasing the amount of your brain that you use to retain and remember the information. Essentially, simply by taking the action of rewriting material in your own words you can virtually double the amount of your brain that you engage in the learning process. That means that you will double your chances of retaining the information, remembering the information, and most importantly, understanding the information.

Putting newly learned information into your own words can also be a critical step in actually understanding the information. No doubt you have seen a movie or TV special that has a coach mentor a student who is struggling with their grades. The trick they always seem to use is to translate the information into a relatable subject for the student. Thus, fractions get translated into football scores, or something similar. Since the student in such movies is usually an athlete, they are able to suddenly understand fractions because they understand the statistics of the sport they play. Needless to say, this is only one example of the overall process of translating information into your own words. The important thing is that you relate to the information you are studying. If you can find a way to interpret newly learned material into a subject you already understand then you don't have to worry about memorizing anything. All you have to do is understand the new terminology for something you have already been using. A good example of this is the analogy of the small army whittling down the large army used to describe breaking down large projects into smaller, more manageable goals. Creating such analogies to embody the information you are learning is a sure way to help you to learn any subject quickly and thoroughly.

Chapter 15: Discipline, Not Motivation

There is a particular phenomenon that happens to a large number of people annually that I personally find to be very strange. A certain amount of time passes (365 days to be exact) and all of a sudden, the people who were seemingly content in letting their lives pass them by, now have the burning desire to finally get going on all of the things they want to accomplish and really should have been doing all along.

"I'm going to get in shape!" Bob yells.

"I'm going to go on that trip!" says Katie.

"I'm going to start doing all of the things I should have been doing last year!" says the random guy whom no one invited.

These are just some of the things people might tell their friends at an average New Year's Eve party. And what exactly do we call these statements? Yup, "New Year's Resolutions".

Now, there probably isn't anything inherently wrong with making these kinds of claims. I agree, there is a certain tangible energy about an impending new year; it carries with it the romantic idea of a fresh start, letting go of the baggage of the previous year, and, in a way, becoming an entirely different person.

What the people making these statements seem to forget however is that, despite having a newfound desire to accomplish their goals, they're still the same person on January 1st that they were on December 31st. As for myself and most likely you probably know, finding the spark to begin the process of bettering your life isn't always easy. It takes a conscious effort to do so, and you could argue that the New Year's resolution might act as that spark, but I've found that it's actually one that usually ends up sputtering out fairly quickly because it relies more on motivation than actual discipline.

So, what's the difference between the two, you ask? Well, as an example, think about two different car owners who buy their vehicles on the exact same day. One of them is named Motivation, and the other goes by Discipline.

Motivation gets his vehicle brand spanking new. It's fresh off the lot, has a full tank of gas, and has that new car smell. It's ready to go. Motivation hops into the driver's seat and, before putting the pedal to the metal, tells himself that he's going to take excellent care of his new baby. At first, everything seems to be going great, but the only problem is that this guy is pretty neglectful of the car, despite the fact that he literally told himself that he would take care of it when he bought it. He doesn't get the oil changed regularly, and he leaves the car outside in the winter for days at a time without starting the engine to warm it up. After enough time goes by, that brand new car starts to break down more often, the mechanics start to wear out, and eventually, the thing stops running at all.

Now, let's take a look at the other car owner: Discipline. On the same day that Motivation was picking up his car from the dealership, Discipline browses the classifieds of his local newspaper and spots an older, used model for sale that has a decent number of miles on it but still runs alright. He picks it up and ends up being the exact opposite type of vehicle owner that Motivation was. Discipline takes the time to change the oil in his car, makes sure to start the car in the winter, and keeps the thing generally well taken care of. A few years down the road (pun intended) when Motivation's car breaks down for the last time and gets towed away to the junkyard, Discipline's used car is sitting at 160,000 miles and runs just as good as the day he picked it up.

And that right there tends to be the biggest difference between motivation and discipline: motivation dwindles while discipline has staying power.

Although motivation can be beneficial in some short-term goals, such as cleaning a room or taking out the trash, it doesn't really translate well to the long term for a few specific reasons that I will outline here:

1. It's a marathon, not a sprint

The largest problem that motivated people must contend with that disciplined people usually don't is the fatigue that usually comes while trying to accomplish something. Usually, when motivation comes to a person, he or she will feel a desire to immediately get started on something they've been putting off for a while. They're going to hit the gym, or they're going to start learning that instrument. And so, with that driving feeling that is so connected to motivation, they take the first necessary step to begin reaching for that goal.

They go out and buy that gym membership or that guitar, and they might even hit the gym pretty hard at first or spend a few hours every week learning chords on that guitar. But, because it was the motivation that spurred them to do these things in the first place, eventually that fire will likely fade unless they can transition their motivated attitude into a disciplined one.

It's a sad truth that for a majority of motivated people – they want to achieve success quickly and without putting in the necessary time to actually attain it. They want to get ripped in the gym or be able to shred killer solos on the guitar without putting in the work that will only get done by someone who is disciplined. Sure, you could probably name a few people who, it would seem, have success coded into their D.N.A. – Jimi Hendrix was a master at the guitar at an early age, but even he spent hours upon hours practicing the craft. The problem with motivation is that it gives people the impression that all they need is a desire to find success in whatever it is they're pursuing when in actuality, this desire needs to be joined at the hip with a disciplined work ethic, and a schedule that is strictly adhered to.

2. It's all in your head

Another big problem with motivation is that it can be unexpectedly deceptive. Going back to the example of a person who gets suddenly motivated to buy a gym membership or a guitar, it is usually the case that the very act of doing these things will fill those people with feelings of great accomplishment.

They might think to themselves, "Wow, I spent real money, which means I'm actually dedicated to following through on this!"

Unfortunately, this is very rarely the case. By taking the first step towards something not because they have a solid plan they can stick to, but rather because they were motivated to do so, mean they aren't seeing the forest for the trees. Sure, buying that gym membership is one of the things a person needs to do before he can start doing solid workouts; but if he goes in there without having a workout plan he can follow, he's most likely going to be doing some random dumbbell curls, maybe running a little bit on a treadmill, and then going home because he wasn't really sure what he needed to do (if it seems like I'm speaking from experience here, it's because I am). He won't be getting in solid workouts, which means he won't start to see any results, and then he'll get discouraged and probably stop going altogether after a certain amount of time without those results.

If, however, this person's approach working out from a disciplined perspective, he'll come up with a solid workout plan and a workout schedule that he'll actually stick with. He'll go into the gym and get this workout done over a period of time, and I can promise you that this person will start to see actual results while the motivated guy just sits at home wondering why those love handles won't take a hike.

3. No time like the present

I don't mean to pick on anyone who has ever made a New Year's resolution. I've done it, my friends and family have done it, and you, dear reader, have more than likely done it. But hopefully, by the end of this chapter, you will have seen the error of your ways, as I have.

The biggest problem with these types of resolutions – besides the fact that they're borne by motivation and will probably not pan out anyway – is that they allow a person to defer bettering themselves by X amount of time. I'm not joking when I say I've literally heard people claim in September that their goal for the new year is to start eating better. What that person actually meant was, "I'm going to allow myself to keep eating an unhealthy diet for the next three and a half months."

It really boggles the mind, for me personally, because most of us know that we need to do some things differently to better ourselves, and yet we say things like "I'll get to it sooner or later" or "Once *blank* changes then I can start to *blank*". I know, I know, it's in our nature to make excuses, but if you really want to be a disciplined person, this is a very bad habit that you need to break.

What you need to come to terms with is that there is no reason not to start doing what you want to do immediately. Because there really is no time like the present. Life is short and unpredictable, and by putting off making yourself better, you are literally giving yourself less time to do so when and if you actually do start the process of doing so.

Despite what you may think, I don't believe that motivation is a totally bad thing. By itself, yes, I do think that it tends to give a person a false perspective of what they need to do and what is expected of them when they begin a new undertaking. But when used in unison with self-discipline, I don't think it's out of the question to say that motivation can be helpful.

For instance, say you just finished a long, stressful day of work, and as you leave the office you remember that on your schedule, you have set a workout. You're so tired, and all you want is to go home and relax; once you're in your car, you actually start to head towards your house instead of the gym. It is here that I think motivation can be of some help. If you try to hype yourself up – motivate yourself – you might find that spark that pushes you to change your mind. Because you're also a disciplined person, you have your workout plan all ready to go, and you're going to continue on your way to reaching your goals.

So, to summarize, motivation has the potential to be harmful when it acts as the spark to start something, but if you're already disciplined, having a little motivation to help you get started on your already scheduled tasks that you know you need to be doing can actually be of some help.

Chapter 16: Using Mnemonics

A mnemonic is a device – usually patterns of letters, associations, or ideas – that help people remember something such as passwords, a list of items, or specialized terms. As a learning or study technique, mnemonics use practically anything under the sun that can assist in recalling or remembering just about anything. Mnemonics helps you accomplish that by assigning pictures or images to particular pieces of information that you want to memorize or learn.

To help you get a better idea of this, let's try out a fun activity that will show you how effective mnemonics can be for learning. Try to memorize or recite the alphabet backwards from Z to A. This means you must memorize the alphabet in reverse order. If you think that's a bit daunting, it's understandable – because it is! If you don't, you're probably a genius.

Here are some ways you can use mnemonics to easily memorize and recite the alphabet backwards and pretty much anything else:

Chunking

This refers to the practice of putting several letters together into more manageable or easier to remember chunks of 3 to 4 letters (or numbers, if you're trying to memorize bank account numbers and the like). It's pretty much the same as trying to devour a big piece of your favorite steak – you don't eat it in just one big bite and swallow! You cut it into small, bite-sized pieces so that you can properly chew, savor, and swallow it until fully consumed. For our reverse alphabet example, you can chunk it this way for easier memorization: ZYXW VUTS RQP ONM LKJ IHG FED CBA

Does this pattern look familiar? Bank corporations use this same method to make it more easy for people to remember their credit card numbers.

Make It Graphic

Ever wondered why the saying "a picture paints a thousand words?" Simple – our minds tend to think visually. That's why it's easier to remember things that are presented to us visually compared to audio or written presentations. For purposes of our reverse-alphabet example, try to associate a graphic or a picture with each of the letters. To make it much easier to recall the letters, make the pictures as wild as possible because the more outrageous they are, the more they'll stand out in your mind and the more you'll be able to recall them with ease. You can apply the same principle for memorizing other things as well.

One of the best application of mnemonics is remembering or memorizing passwords or codes. Let's take a look at examples of passwords or codes and how you can use mnemonics to easily remember or memorize them:

☐   ihavbn = I Have A Very Big Nose

☐   pmnia = Picking My Nose Is Awesome

Chapter 17: Hearing and Listening Skills to Improve Your Memory

We have already discussed how good listening skills boost your overall focus and in turn your memory. To reiterate, when you keenly listen to something, you effectively and successfully encode that auditory information, and when you constantly focus on it, you turn it into long-term memory that you can easily retrieve from your memory bank anytime you want.

To ensure you effectively listen to things when required, here are some tactics you can try.

Face the source of auditory input and focus on it

If you are constantly fidgeting while listening to something, be it a friend sharing his/her story with you, a presenter giving a speech on a seminar you are attending, or a podcast on how to achieve your goals, you will not be able to listen to it attentively.

Remember, information received from different senses related to a similar topic often becomes a blended well that helps consolidate the information better. That said, if you receive different stimuli related to diverse topics, you will only jumble up everything and create chaos in your brain. Before you realize it, you will feel exhausted and unable to focus on anything at all.

When listening to something or someone, do not fidget with anything at all; face the auditory source such as your MP3 player, TV, or the speaker directly and maintain eye contact with it even if it is a non-living object. Facing the object/person directly means you will not keep looking here and there; you will focus on it keenly. This helps you build and sustain focus on the auditory source, hold on to every word that reaches your ears, process the information effectively, and encode the information perfectly.

Reduce background noise

Whether it is the vacuum cleaner constantly humming in the background or the blender buzzing away on full speed, if there is any background noise while you are trying to listening to something, you will not pay attention to it well.

To ensure that you attentively listen to the information you are trying to absorb, reduce any background noise, and try to cut it off completely. This is possible when you have control over the environment such as your own house or office. However, if you share the space with someone, you can request others to cut back on the unnecessary noise for some time, use noise cancelation technologies, or work when you are alone.

Ask questions

Sometimes you may be unable to memorize something easily because you do not understand it well even if you are hearing it just fine. Good listening skills are more than just keenly listening to something; they also require you to comprehend the matter properly because when you understand something fully, you encode the information effectively and transfer it to your long-term storage faculties. An excellent way to accomplish this very goal is to ask questions when listening to something.

If, for example, you are having a conversation with a board partner, potential business investor, friend, colleague, or anyone else about a subject important to you and one you would like to remember details, ask the person different deep and meaningful questions about it. Pay attention to what the person says and then ask thoughtful questions keeping in mind the context of the conversation as well as the goal you and the other person are trying to achieve.

Likewise, if you are listening to a lecture, podcast, video or audio program that you would like to learn from and commit to your memory, write down any important questions that pop up in your head and explore their answers later. Once you are clear about a certain concept, it will deeply imbed in your mind and become a part of your long-term memories.

Picturize

As described earlier in the book, when you picture something in your mind, you focus better on it. Use this technique to immerse yourself in the experience, and to open your ears and mind to listening attentively. While listening to something, do not just hear with your ears; also see with your mind. Whatever you are listening to, create a vivid mental model of it in your head.

Pay attention to the phrases, important keywords, pointers, and elements and use them to create a mental sketch and focus on it. When you visualize things while hearing them, you compel your brain to focus harder on the topic, become engaged in the experience, and encode the information better. Effective encoding leads to solid consolidation and successful retrieval of that information.

Maintain a curious, nonjudgmental, open mind

When we listen to someone or something such as a video, we do more than just listen with our ears; we also listen with the preconceived notions stuck in our head.

We judge everything we listen to based on our individual superficial desires, societal norms and clichés, and preconceived notions. This clouds our objective thinking and unbiased state of mind, and while we may think we make independent, logical decisions, we are often just paying heed to biased information.

Sound, informed decisions that play out well for you in the long-term and help you feel happy and content from within can only come from a sane, logical, accepting, and nonjudgmental state of mind. To make this happen, you need to listen with an open mind.

When you listen to something, you do not jump to conclusions; you never put labels on anything. If any preconceived notion pops up and tries to dictate, remind yourself of your job to listen clearly and nonjudgmentally, and realign your attention to the conversation.

Write down important points if you have to and analyze the information as objectively as possible. This helps you perceive things for what they are, dig deeper into things with clarity and comprehend the truth to the maximum extent. As you understand things better, you are able to remember them clearly as well.

Try LACE

LACE (Listening and Communication Enhancement) is a software program specifically created to improve your listening skills. It comprises of five dissimilar listening skills designed to accelerate your listening, communication, and cognitive abilities. These include the following:

Processing quick speech

Picking out one particular voice from a noisy environment

Filling missing words in a conversation

Improving auditory memory

Focusing on one particular voice in a cornucopia of voices.

You can find out more about LACE here. Once you wrap your head around how it works, use the program regularly to yield desired outcomes.

Spaced repetition

You are likelier to remember something you heard yesterday than something you heard a few months ago. In psychology, we call this the 'forgetting curve.' It happens because our short-term memory does not extend over a long period. Limited to just a few seconds to sometimes a couple of minutes, our working memories fade when we do not reinforce the respective ideas. Spaced repetition is a fantastic technique that reinforces your memory and keeps that from happening.

When you listen to something, you must do it attentively and after a few seconds, try to recall what you heard or read. You can then use flashcards or repeat the concepts verbally to test your memory and repeat the technique several times spaced with 2 to 5 minute intervals in between.

Slowly, increase the space between the repetitions and do it after a 10-minute gap. Try this for 20 to 30 minutes with important and complex information and for 10 minutes with relatively simpler information; you will quickly commit it to your long-term memory.

Try mnemonics

Mnemonics are amazing memory improvement tools that assist in information consolidation and retention. They utilize elaborative encoding, imagery, and retrieval cues to help you acquire information quickly, commit it to your memory, and then retrieve it when required.

While we have many different kinds of mnemonics, some of which we shall discuss in other chapters, here, we will stick to musical mnemonics and acronyms only as they relate closely to listening and speaking.

Acronyms are short abbreviations of relatively longer phrases, string of words, an entire sentence, or sometimes a longer sentence or phrase to remember an idea or a series of words/concepts. For instance, 'Every Good Boy Does Fine' is a popular acronym to memorize the treble clef: EGBDF. Similarly, the Great Lakes: Huron, Ontario, Michigan, Erie, and

Superior become the common acronym 'HOMES.'

Every time you want to memorize a complex piece of information, create a fun acronym around it and then chant it repeatedly, aloud, and clear so that you imbed it in your mind and transfer it to your long-term memory. You can also create a fun, entertaining jingle around something you are trying to memorize and sing it out loudly. While you do that, use the other techniques too so that you can better commit it to memory. For instance, visualize what you are saying, practice spaced repetition, and listen to it nonjudgmentally to improve your understanding of concepts.

Mention names, things etc. in a conversation

If you are talking to someone and would like to memorize his/her name or any other piece of information or detail related to him/her, mention that thing several times in the conversation. If you would like to remember that Janet whom you just met at a conference is a speech therapist and has an office in Boston, mention her name a few times in the conversation and ask questions about her practice.

Similarly, if you would like to memorize the rules of public speaking you just learned in a presentation given by a colleague, engage the colleague in a conversation about it, and repeat the rules a few times.

Mentioning things repeatedly helps that information sink into your memory, which makes it easier for you to retain and retrieve it when needed.

Record yourself

To get a better hang of what you are memorizing, record yourself as you do it. Keep a tape recorder or record yourself in your phone's recorder to keep track of all the facts/figures you speak of. You then need to listen to your recording repeatedly, and rehearse the speech or information aloud.

When you go through an account repeatedly, it sinks deeper into your memory better and turns into your long-term memories.

Chapter 18: Ineffective Techniques and Learning Myths- How NOT to Train the Brain

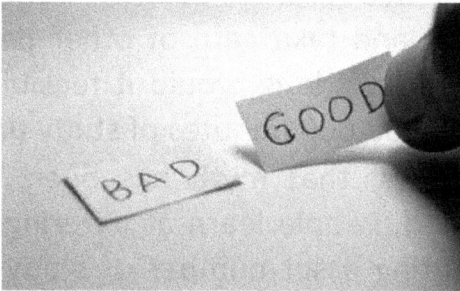

While there are lot of correct ways to train the brain, study and practice well, and commit to learning new skills, there are also a lot of myths and techniques that are ineffective, or worse, even harmful. It's important to stay the course and stick to your good study habits, so as not to fall into any of these bad habits or be taken in by myths.

The 10,000-Hour Rule

For many years, the 10,000-hour rule was used to determine expertise. The rule states that one must put 10,000 hours of study or practice into a skill to be considered a master. That's a lot of time- if you studied 24 hours a day, you'd have to study for nearly 417 days straight to become considered an expert. Given that humans need to eat, sleep, work, raise children, and take care of other personal business, how long would it feasibly take to get in 600,000 minutes of study time?

These days, that myth has been largely debunked. People learn at differing paces and putting a set number of study hours on any skill has become outdated. Yes, some certifications and professional qualifications still require a set number of hours on a task to be considered competent, but the old rule has mostly been abandoned.

More recently, experts have suggested it's better to get outside input to determine your own mastery. Find a mentor, tutor, or coach to help you gauge your competency on your chosen subject. Feedback can give you guidance on where you need to improve and what you can consider 'learned material', and shape the next phase of your learning experience.

Choosing Sides

Another myth that's been afloat for years is that of a person being strictly right- or left-brained, and that this was determined by dominant hand usage. This has lent credence to the theory that left-handed, right-brained people are more creative and artsy, and right-handed, left-brained people are more analytical. This theory is highly inaccurate.

The truth is, we all use both sides of our brains equally, so there is no need to categorize yourself based on a notion of using one side of the brain more effectively. Lefties- you can go ahead and learn some advanced math! Righties, go out and get yourself some art supplies!

The 10% Myth

Another tall tale about how we use our brains is the myth that says we only use about 10 percent of the capacity of our brains. Evidence now shows that humans, over the course of a day, use 100 percent of their brain matter, perhaps just not all at once. This means, unfortunately, that there's no superpowers to be had when the brain is fully unlocked, as some pop culture tropes would suggest. We'd be better off seeking out radioactive spiders and cosmic clouds to become superheroes.* Researchers now say that how we study has a greater effect on brain development than what we study. Remember, the brain is an ever evolving organ, and it is constantly firing and rewiring.

*Disclaimer- that was a comic book joke. Please don't expose yourself to dangerous substances or circumstances in the pursuit of superpowers!

Building a Pyramid

Just like there are abundant theories on how the Great Pyramids were built at Giza, no one is exactly sure where the Learning Pyramid theory arose. The Learning Pyramid theory states that a person retains information in percentages: 10 percent of things they've read, 20 percent of the things they've heard, 30 percent of the things they've seen, 50 percent of the things they've seen AND heard, 70 percent of the things they've said or written, and

90 percent of the things they have done or taught to others.

Frankly, this just isn't true, and you shouldn't base your study habits on the learning pyramid. Education experts say that this theory is total nonsense, and the percentage numbers themselves cannot be backed up with biology or neuroscience.

Intelligence is a Fixed Point

Intelligence, and how we perceive intelligence, plays a major factor in how we learn. Despite what we might have once thought, intelligence is NOT determined at birth. Yes, people can get smarter. Raw intelligence has been measured in IQ (intelligence quotient) since the first tests were introduced in the early part of the twentieth century. These tests are designed to measure not what you've learned, but what you have the capacity to learn.

There's been a move away from raw IQ scores recently because they don't tell the whole story of a person's capabilities, and recent studies prove that intelligence can actually be increased through study. For a long time, students were classified on their perceived intelligence levels, and many lower IQ students were treated as if they did not have the capacity to improve themselves. We now know this to be untrue.

The flip side of this is using high IQ to motivate students. It often backfires; when a student is praised for simply 'being smart', they don't believe that they need to study to learn. This often results in poor study habits and disappointing results when those same students get to institutions of higher learning. Those students may still be the smart kids, but the students who work hard are the ones who will achieve goals and be offered opportunities.

The middle ground here would seem to be to focus on small, attainable goals that all work toward the desired end result, and to not let others develop misconceptions based on your intelligence. Don't let yourself develop misconceptions about your own intelligence, either! Learn to praise yourself and others for the effort put into learning, not simply for IQ.

Going with Your Gut

Always go with your first answer! Remember that from middle school multiple choice tests? Actually, don't do that. While it was long believed that your brain would involuntarily spit out the needed information on the first try, that's not completely true. It takes critical thinking skills to go back and review your answers on an exam or quiz. There's no scientific evidence to suggest that your first answer is any more likely to be correct than an answer you come up with after second thoughts. That first gut-reaction answer isn't necessarily wrong, but if you can, analyze your answers to determine if they're correct.

While the above advice applies more to formal learning settings, it can be applied to adult learning or independent learning situations, too. Critical thinking is a key component in being a strong learner, and being able to critique yourself is a great way to gauge yourself against the standard. If you've got a mentor or tutor, they may also likely administer some form of testing to determine your progress, and therefore you'll want to keep your test-taking skills sharp.

One Thing at a Time?

The old standard was that learning methods had to be singular and focused to be effective. That's not quite true, and in fact, we learn much better when we mix up the routine. Inside our schools today, teachers are using multi-media approaches to learning, and as an adult learner, you can apply these concepts for yourself, too.

When you're studying, don't lock yourself into a routine so tight that you become bored and lose motivation. While it's important to reinforce your learning material, do so with a mix of reading, visual aids, and film. Try occasionally changing up your location- study outside on a nice day, or set up different backgrounds on your computer. Sometimes a change of pace is needed to reset your brain. Remember, one of the goals is to keep your mind active enough to maintain plasticity. No one wants to feel as if they've become stagnant.

Imitation is the Greatest Form of Flattery

While that may or may not be true, what certainly isn't true is that imitating or emulating the experts will help you learn faster. The people who know the most about the things you want to learn are great resources, but it took them plenty of study and hard work to get to where they are. Simply copying them will not gain you any true knowledge.

Instead, take a look at their body of work and use it as study material. Most advanced learners, like college professors or scientific professionals, are published in journals or have written books. There are experts in every field who regularly publish in trade magazines. Look at where they are sourcing their own material, find out what their path to knowledge was, and pick and choose the pieces that can help you advance in your own studies. The simple fact is that you, a beginner, cannot learn at the same rate as them, the experts, but this a matter of proficiency. We all need to learn at an appropriate pace and that pace is based on our own experiences.

How to Avoid the Myths and Make Friends with Time

In this discussion of the good, the bad, and the inaccurate of learning methods and study habits, we've touched upon the T-word, TIME, a few times. It's important to set aside time for studying and practice, but life has a way of piling up obligations. With limited periods available to study, how can that time be effectively managed? In the next chapter, we'll take a look at how to focus your efforts and maximize study time to reach your goals.

Chapter 19: Surround Yourself with the Right People

Another variable to consider when studying is whether you should study alone or with a group. Some people will swear that the only way you can concentrate on the material you are studying is to study in absolute solitude. Others contend that the energy and encouragement of others is critical in staying on track with the task at hand. Again, different people respond to certain environmental factors in different ways, so there is no real right or wrong answer to this question. The important thing to do is to determine which conditions are best for you. Only then can you hope to improve the results of your study efforts, thereby increasing the amount of information you master in a shorter period of time.

In the case of studying with a group there are several variables which need to be considered to ensure that you get the most for your time and energy. First you need to make sure that the group you study with conforms to your personal study needs. As mentioned in the previous chapters you might find that you require silence while studying, or that you might prefer ambient noise. The time of day and the location where you study are also very relevant in terms of how productive your study sessions prove to be. If you choose to study with other people then you need to make sure that they fit into these categories in a way that is beneficial to you. It makes no sense to study with a group of people who are loud if you require silence in order to concentrate. Additionally, it would be catastrophic to study with a group who insisted on eating while studying as this would reduce the results of your efforts. Therefore, even if you decide that studying with a group is a good thing for you it is critical that you find the right group for your needs. Finding likeminded people will go a long way to helping you to learn any subject more quickly and effectively.

The second thing to consider when studying with a group of people is their motivation. Some groups will be highly motivated to study and focus on the material at hand, whereas others might be a little more laid back, choosing to mix studying with having a good time. At first glance it might seem like a simple decision to make. After all, how can you go wrong by picking the people who are wholly focused on studying and learning? The fact of the matter is that the study only group can actually be the wrong choice, depending on which energy suits your personality. The energy of the group is all important when choosing a group to study with. People who focus solely on studying may actually cause you to become more stressed while studying, as they don't allow for blowing off steam during the process. In this case the group that mixes work and pleasure might be right for you. Ultimately you want to feel as relaxed and confident as possible while studying, thus the group needs to contribute toward those feelings in a real way. Taking the time to experiment with different groups will help you to know which group dynamic works best for you.

A trap that many people fall into is that they assume that spending time with smarter people is the right thing to do. For some people this might be true, but there is a lot to be said for spending time with people of like intellect or even lower intellect than you. In the case of people who are equal to you in terms of intelligence these people will often have similar questions and issues to the ones you encounter. Thus, spending time with these people can be highly advantageous as it will enable you to overcome the problems you face with others in the same boat. Alternatively, you may find that you can offer help to the other members of the group as a result of having solved similar problems in the past. The bottom line is that likeminded people can make any situation easier to handle just by sharing the experience from the same perspective.

Spending time with persons of a slightly less intellectual level than you can also be very helpful. While this seems counter intuitive at first there is actually a very rational explanation to this notion. When you study with people slightly less intelligent or learned in the particular subject than yourself you will be in a position to help them understand certain things. In the event that you can answer the questions they have that will allow you to practice the information you have learned. By teaching others you will increase your own understanding of the subject, which will enable you to more easily absorb the new information you are learning. If you constantly spend time with people smarter than yourself then you can find yourself constantly struggling to keep up. Rather than being able to answer questions you might be the only one asking any. This is counterproductive to effective learning as it never gives you the chance to put your knowledge to good use.

Chapter 20: How To Learn The German Language Fast

The desire to enhance your knowledge or to find a better job, traveling abroad, opening new horizons and personal development are the most common motives for learning a new language. However, when we try to learn it, it turns out that we can find a lot of obstacles on the path to fulfilling your dreams. Lack of time to learn, slow progress or lack of faith in the effectiveness, eventually deprive us of enthusiasm and motivation. These problems concern most of us, but especially adults, who are often convinced that learning at their age no longer makes sense.

If you are one of these people, heads up! There are some methods that will allow you to learn any foreign language in a short period of time. Nowadays, speaking foreign languages like the German is the foundation of everything. This can open new doors for you, get you a good job or promotion. In addition, knowledge of just one foreign language is incredibly useful. This opens many doors, thanks to which we can go explore new things.

Learning more about the culture of the people speaking the German language is without doubt the best way to learn this foreign language. This means that you should surround yourself with people and culture of the language you want to learn. The best way to do that is to sign up to a German languages courses or use a software for learning (which will help you learn the languages faster). Finally, a very important factor in language learning is to spend enough time surrounded by people who talk that language. The key is to continue to invest enough time and effort.

Listen to the language by watching the news, television dramas and movies. It is a big plus if you find a group of people who speak that language. The next thing you can do is read. Reading helps you focus on words and language structures.

Pay attention to the pronunciation, gestures and facial expressions when a word is being pronounced. With the verbal part of language learning, we often neglect the nonverbal part of learning a foreign language which also plays an important role. Mastering the non-verbal aspect will help you reach an advanced level of knowledge of the language.

Be patient while learning. It takes time and effort. The brain will slowly begin to understand the different aspects, rules and structure of the language.

Finally, the time and effort spent on learning the German language will pay off in the long run.

Accelerated Learning of Spanish

Learning has never been as efficient throughout human history as it is now. Thanks to accelerated learning, we now have the potential to expand our knowledge quicker than we do now. Of course, the amount that an individual decides to learn is still completely up to them. One of the first things that was taught at an accelerated pace was languages. In 1970, Suggestopedia was created, which was a type of learning that was used to help people learn languages at a quicker pace. The environment and teaching were considered the most important aspects when it came to learning, and still is.

Learning Spanish

Spanish is considered one of the easiest languages to learn. It is also the second most spoken language in the world, and probably the language most spoken around the world. It is said that Spanish can be learnt in around six months if spoken everyday. Although this sounds like not much time at all when compared to other languages, it is still possible to learn this language in half of that time if accelerated learning is applied to it. Accelerated learning involves high intensity and focused learning. It offers you a great learning environment, which is probably the most important thing when it comes to learning quickly and effectively.

Important Aspects

Although it sounds all good and amazing to apply accelerated learning to learning to language, it is much easier said than done. The main disadvantage of accelerated learning is that it is much more stressful than learning something at an average pace. You are analyzing more information at a much shorter pace, which is bound to take its toll on your brain. You need to make sure that you prepare your brain for this increased influx of information.

Self-Motivation

Make sure that you try your best to motivate yourself. One thing about accelerated learning is that it requires you to have a strong sense of self discipline. You need to take control of those bad urges to be lazy, and only think about being productive.

Use all your Senses

Try to expose all of your senses to the language, this will help the brain learn easier and therefore accelerate the speed at which you retain information. Spanish is a perfect example because they are passionate when they speak, you can feel them speaking. Be expressive and give yourself to the language.

Planning

One of the most important things in life is to plan. Failing to plan is planning to fail. This idea is much more important when applying accelerated learning to something. You need to plan what you are going to get to learn everyday and compromise or you'll just end up falling behind and you'll lose control of what's going on and give up.

Chapter 21: Computer Role in Accelerated Learning

Accelerated Learning

Accelerated learning is the way forward. It is the best way to learn in this day and age, where everything happens at such at such a rapid pace. If everything else is so fat, why shouldn't the rate at which we learn to be quick as well? It only makes sense, really. Computers are the one of the key reasons why the world has sped up. The internet and electronic devices in general have enabled us as a race to communicate with people across the other sides of the world in seconds. Computers also have helped us learn quicker. Here are a few ways that computers have helped accelerate the rate at which we learn.

Everything you need to Know, in One Place

The great thing about a computer is that it holds literally everything you will ever need to learn within itself or on the internet. This is important, because before computers it was considered difficult to accumulate all the information that you needed to efficiently learn something. Learning used to be a slow process, but thanks to computers and accelerated learning, this is no longer the case. Forget having to look through dozens of books to simply find a few points that you are looking for. With computers, simply search what you are wondering and it is likely that you'll find the information and understand it within minutes.

Computer's Accelerate Learning

Perhaps a key example of how computers can speed up the way that we learn is through watching YouTube videos. The videos offer two of your senses the opportunity to learn something. You get to hear something and see it. Although you could already do this if you had a teacher, with videos and YouTube you can learn whatever you want efficiently and effectively without ever having to interact with anyone else. Accelerated learning and computers have helped people build an independence when it comes to their learning.

Computer's Role

A computer's role in accelerated learning is to literally accelerate it. If you want to learn slowly and like everyone else, you will follow the mainstream and go to class, learn from a teacher with people who aren't really passionate about what they are being taught. The quality of learning is low and slow. With computers, it gives you the opportunity to only rely on yourself. When you are only relying on yourself, you dictate the quality as well as the amount of time it takes to learn. Computers allow you to accelerate your learning as quickly as you want to.

Chapter 22: The Case for Learning at Work

Business owners seem to be showing more interest in what their staff has to offer. Because of the new economy, organizations need to continue learning to keep their heads above the water.

Learning is a raw material that requires creative application in order to be transformed into a useful competitive resource. Continuous learning across all departments is as important as lifeblood that needs to continue flowing if the organization is to stay alive.

The more knowledge we have about ourselves, the market we operate in as well as about the way we run things, the better equipped we will be to provide better services to our clients, staff, investors, and others.

To stay competitive, you need to be at the top of the learning ladder, flowing with the latest trends to meet up with the demands of your customers.

Most leaders are aware of the fact that we live in a world that keeps changing rapidly. Hence, there is a constant need for smart and flexible minds that can adapt to these changes. We are yet to exploit one-fifth of our true potential, with the right training, and enabling environment, the sky is just the beginning for such bright minds.

We must be able to apply what we've learned to strategize our business. This is imperative considering the rapid changes that occur in the business world. After learning something new, there is a great need for you to be flexible in order to be in tune with the new trends in the fast-changing business environment. It matters because the sector is fast-changing. Learning involves being flexible and having minds that can manage this kind of fast-moving environment. All employees need to be open-minded and blend fast.

Companies involved in providing services for the clients have a greater need to keep on learning.

Both flexibility and adaptability are equally important because service providing companies are on the increase daily, thus the need for them to be really flexible and adaptable if they want to stay competitive. In summary, to keep providing satisfactory and valuable services, learning is sine qua non.

Six Benefits of Learning

There are about six reasons that all business owners must make learning a habit. Each of these six points is related to the other. This applies to individuals and big business owners. They are the following:

1. Productivity. Your productivity and the quality of your services can be greatly enhanced by learning and adapting to new trends as soon as possible. Hence, the need for flexibility

2. Competitive advantage. You will be better than your rivals. Learning can give you an edge above your competitors thereby helping you survive in the business world. While most businesses that fail to learn are folding up, your business will float above the tides of obstacles.

Customer's feedback is therefore very important in order to know areas where business owners need to adjust or improve. In some businesses, the needs of the customers are obvious while others need to make concerted efforts to get feedbacks. When the staff goes further to learn and acquire more qualifications, it gives them a competitive advantage and put them in line for a promotion.

3. More knowledge. One of the major problems that most organizations face is not the lack of knowledge but how to put these resources into good use. According to an American scholar Warren Bennis, who stated that "the main problem most leaders of the twenty-first-century face is how to maximize the brainpower within their organizations." In practice, this entails understanding that most things that organizations and individuals know remain at an implicit level too often. Some of these brainpowers remain at a particular level for years and that way, such knowledge remain stagnant rather than flowing through all the system of

such an organization. For instance, a group that was involved in a successful project must have learned one new thing or the other which others not belonging to the group need to learn as well; if not, such brainpower and their knowledge will be mere waste. For example, if you know how to drive, you just get in and drive you might not see the need to sit down and take a moment to think about how to drive until you need to teach your son or daughter how to drive. That is when you think of ways to carefully instruct such ones. This is the case for brainpower. This is known as knowledge management.

When it comes to knowledge management, there are about three assumptions:

It is a new phenomenon.

It is all about computer systems.

Knowledge cannot be managed.

The only way to acquire knowledge is through learning. Once you learn and understand something new, you've just gained a new insight. Then, you need to share that insight with others. Thus, the willingness of individuals to learn, the rate at which they learn and the way they apply what they learned will determine their success in life.

4. Change. The twentieth century witnessed predictable trends of inventions which lasted for many years. Except for the rate at which a company is learning is much faster than the rate at which external changes are occurring, it will be difficult if not impossible for such businesses to survive. Learning rapidly is therefore imperative for survival, hence the need to be flexible and adaptable. Multitalented employees are needed in every organization, to keep adding value to the business. Fast learning is imperative for survival. This is also applicable to your personal life as well. How well you handle with an unforeseen event such as a divorce or loss of a mate or parent and others will be determined by your sense of adaptability which you've acquired over time.

5. Learning as a key to progressive cultural changes. Most times, people ordered to

do something in a way that is totally different without giving proper instructions. But if you take time to explain the reasons that the change is necessary, you will be helping them learn new things, and they will be more willing to be a part of such a change.

6. Learning motivates. Most employees appreciate employers that encouraged them to keep learning. According to a poll that was carried out in 1998, "About 77 percent of those interviewed said they prefer a boss that encouraged learning but pays less over one who pays more but does not support the employees in terms of learning." Those employees who took their time to improve on themselves by learning can relate how motivated they were by the things they learned.

Learning benefits everyone, both the individual and the organization at large. Holding to this fact, the British government established an individual learning account (ILA). This was set up to encourage individuals to save up toward their learning just as they do for other projects such as a house, health insurance, pension, vacation, etc. The scheme is more like a virtual economy or a savings bond and those who saved can enjoy a tax deduction or a rebate of about 80 percent on the total amount spent on learning. The discount can be as much as £400 yearly and is paid back at the point of payment. With ILA anyone can pay for a lifelong educational program. Another interesting fact is that those who operate this type of account could receive support from a 3rd party such as a parent, grandparent, an employer, etc.

If every country in the world could adapt this method of paid education, the globe will be filled with individuals who are addicted to learning such a world will indeed be a better place. You can learn anything you wish to learn.

Chapter 23: Learning management is project management

A) Study as a project

The points addressed in this book so far for effective learning may have already been fully or at least partially. It is important to internalize these points, because they are prepared to do so, this knowledge about the subject of learning completely automatically and is already unconsciously prepared for the mentioned pitfalls. The above should therefore have been embedded in your subconscious, so to speak as a knowledge base for learning.

The previous chapter (**Chapter 4: Learning Methods**) has taught you very concrete practical tips on learning methods that they can directly apply and which will help them to learn the relevant subject as effectively as possible. Now that they are aware of the topic of learning and have prepared themselves mentally for it and are equipped with practical help for learning, it can finally start.

But no! Take a little moment - quite in the sense of a good preparation - for a much too often forgotten but essential thing: Let us come to the possibly decisive turning point on the way to a successful study. Unfortunately this point is too often simply forgotten. What is meant is that

"Learning or self-management"

Behind the concept of learning management are not dry facts, as one might think. It is not a matter of praying down here, how they should divide their time, what materials they should use and what lecture they should attend. Learning management is the underlying philosophy, its attitude, its personal life plan.

They have deliberately decided to study. And they combine hopes and goals with this course. It is not a hobby, which one times times tried and also no short-lived New Year's set. If it does not work, not too bad. No, they want it, and as successful as possible. That's why they may be among those who already have a _{great} _{head} start over fellow students. While most of them are plunging into the cold water, they are already thinking, researching and informing themselves with texts like this here to increase their effectiveness in their studies. This shows: They take the degree seriously!

The enterprise

This chapter is based on the last sentence. Take his studies seriously - that is the basis. Imagine that they are in the process of building, managing, managing their own business. The success of her company is her very personal project, to which she devotes almost all her attention. They lead their employees, react to sales figures, plan campaigns, enter into negotiations, hire new employees - in short: they are their company, that is their project.

A company called Study

Now they do not run a fictitious company, they do their studies. Her studies are her own personal project. You alone determine the quality of the product, the marketing, the resources and the upcoming appointments. The success of their project is dependent on their decisions, their plans, the way they lead the project, how they manage the project alone as their boss. So you are the project leader, your own project manager. All responsibility lies with them.

The project manager

From now on they have to see themselves as project managers. Not the lecturers are responsible for the success of their project. Solve it from the notion that she is holding someone by the hand, and if they always do well, what the one says and applies to them, they will be completely automatic. Only they know their work and everyday life. Only they know their personal goal that they want to achieve and their very individual ambitions in this regard. Above all, they only know the resources at their disposal, namely their energy.

B) The project plan

No company works, if the management simply loses control, here and there decisions are made, as they are just now

the hot phase just before examinations? What material possibilities for the appropriation of the material can they use (events of the university, university documents, Internet, books, scripts, etc.)?

·Analyze yourself in terms of learning itself. What type of learning are they? Which channels are best suited for receiving material? What are the best learning methods? Should they set up a learning group or do they prefer to study alone? How often do they have to repeat so that the new fabric sits? What are their weaknesses (eg in the examination technique, the application of knowledge, the memorization, the abstract content, etc.)? How quickly do they absorb new fabric in general, how many repetitions do they need to feel safe?

On the basis of the answers to these (and more, more detailed, the better) questions, they should create their project plan. Plan to do so in a way that is not as good as kickbacks, and if necessary, create a " Plan B " and a crisis or emergency   plan . Be   self-critical, realistic and prepared. This is their project, their goal, they alone want to achieve it. So they take responsibility for perfect planning.

C) Be your own project manager

Specifically,

They must be self-responsible and active in their studies. This is especially true of their learning strategy. How effective they are learning determines how successful their studies are. The danger is great to slip into the passivity and to perceive the material more and more through passive channels. Depths are almost always the triggers to sway the study because you were not prepared for it and can be pulled down by negative emotions.

At such moments, they have to say again and again:

.This is my project, I am the project manager - then I will find a solution!

No one will write the required exams for them, no one will learn the stuff for them. The responsibility and choice of the weapons (ie the material, the learning method, the project plan, etc.) is with them. For this, however, they will sooner or later reap the laurels for their hard work.

TIP : You are your own boss. Now, keep in mind that their studies are their own personal project and they decide on their own success. Be your self-responsible, forward-looking, strategic project leader.

CONCLUSION

Exercising your brain to think like a scientist involves three things: the ability to pay attention to unexpected findings instead of rejecting them, methodological reasoning and the ability to look beyond a simple answer. When dealing with numbers, it is possible to train the brain towards scientific based goal orientation, whereby, one tries to explain surprising results or inferences from experiments.

Human nature means that we draw on our past experiences and existing knowledge when analyzing and explaining any results. When you choose to think like a scientist, you learn to avoid distorting results by looking for evidence that is consistent with your existing knowledge. Your focus should change to being open to unexpected findings.

Exercise your brain by changing your approach to problems. Rather than viewing problems as a barrier, view them as opportunities that open up for further discovery.

Problem solving should be your focus, rather than avoidance or frustration. If you are working on a problem, and you seem unable to find a solution, identify methods available that will allow you to further analyses the results. To think like a scientist, you should open up your mind to more experiences, and in turn explore methods to build on these experiences.

Remember that the scientist always pursue more than one solution, so evaluate your results in a way that you can get information that represents different points of view.

Exercising your brain will let you reap huge profits from having the right attitude for numbers. It is not so complicated, which you must have figured out after reading this book.

Happy Thinking!